SEVENTH SON OF A SEVENTH SON

Seventh Son
of a
Seventh Son

THE LIFE STORY OF A HEALER

Finbarr Nolan
with
Martin Duffy

MAINSTREAM
PUBLISHING

First published in Great Britain 1992 by
MAINSTREAM PUBLISHING COMPANY (EDINBURGH) LTD
7 Albany Street
Edinburgh EH1 3UG

ISBN 1 85158 414 5

A catalogue record for this book is available from the British Library

Typeset in 11 pt Baskerville by
Seton Music Graphics Ltd, Ireland

Printed in Great Britain by
Mackays of Chatham PLC, Chatham

All the people who appear in this book are referred to by their real names with
the exception of Jack Harte who, for personal reasons, requested that his name
be changed.

*I dedicate this book
to
my mother
in gratitude for her strength, her support,
and her inspiration*

CONTENTS

FOREWORD

In Irish folklore there are many kinds of people born with special powers. There's the child that never saw its own father, or the child born with a caul, or the child whose parents had the same surname before marriage, or the child born on a Sunday. Most particularly, however, the seventh son or seventh daughter has special powers. The seventh son is said to be able to cure ringworm, or 'running worm' as it is sometimes known, and the seventh daughter can cure worms.

Belief in the special gifts of a seventh son or daughter can be found in folklore throughout the world. Leslie Shepard, in his *Encyclopedia of Occultism and Parapsychology*, states that in Romania the seventh child is fated to become a vampire, and that in England in the seventeenth century there were reports of a seventh son healing the deaf, blind and lame. In France, the seventh son was called a *Marcou* and branded

9

with a fleur-de-lis. The *Marcou* breathed on the affected part, or the patient touched his fleur-de-lis.

These gifts are steeped in many odd traditions. It is said, for instance, that for a seventh son to be initiated into his power he must have a worm bandaged on to each hand when he is born and the worms must be kept there until they die. Most healers believe that they mustn't be thanked for what they do, and it is also thought that overuse of the gift will lead to its loss.

The application of the healing differs from place to place. Nearly always, it is the laying of the right hand on the affected part that brings the cure, while the sign of the cross is also made over the patient and sometimes prayers said. Some, however, breathe over the affected area. Others use their saliva, and one Irish seventh son blessed soil which was then mixed with water and applied to the affected area. There are those who say the power only works between sunrise and sunset on certain specified days, while others acknowledge no such restriction.

Local history in Longford tells of a seventh son in a Daly family who was known simply as "the doctor". The Irish Folklore Department of University College Dublin has in its records the recollections of Michael O'Suilleabhain, who was a seventh son and cured many people during his life. He would put the thumb of his right hand in his mouth and then make the sign of the cross with it on the affected part. He would do this on three separate days, and he said he cured many ailments including what he referred to as "the evil", though he said he couldn't cure "bone evil".

The ability to heal was once seen as the mark of greatness, and in France and England there was a healing known as the Royal Touch. Ringworm was known in England and France as "the king's evil", being an ailment that royalty could heal by touch. In the seventeenth century Charles II, re-establishing royalty in England after the civil war, touched as many as 100,000 subjects in his campaign to show he had the gift of the Royal Touch. At that time, however, there was a healer in Ireland named Valentine Greatrakes who healed vast numbers of people and undermined the king by his gift. Greatrakes said that his gift was revealed to him in three visions in which God granted him the right to act as a healer on His behalf.

Good luck was also said to attend the seventh child. In olden days, when captains of merchant ships were setting sail on long voyages, they would try to have a seventh son on the ship. Legend had it that the ship wouldn't sink with a seventh son on board.

The seventh son of a seventh son or the seventh daughter of a seventh daughter are the jewels in the crown of folk-healing. They are said to have the power of second sight, and fortune-telling, and to be able to cure any illness. Leslie Shepard, in his *Encyclopedia* mentioned above, says, "There was a general belief in Britain that the seventh son of a seventh son was destined to be a physician, having an intuitive knowledge of the art of healing, often curing a patient simply by touching the afflicted part."

The reason why the seventh child – as opposed to the first or fifth, for example – should have special powers must have its roots in ancient beliefs. The number seven has many mystical and religious associations. Apart from the Bible's telling of God creating the world in seven days, the number features throughout the Old and New Testaments. Seven is a very significant number in numerology and is the basic unit of transition in natural cycles from the week as a phase of the lunar cycle to the idea that many of life's patterns are divided in phases of seven.

Healing and religion are, of course, deeply linked. Jesus Christ healed the sick and the lame, and many saints were healers. Jesus said that others could heal in His name and through His power, and the hope of healing through prayer is a growing force in Christian religions. There are those who believe that healers have the gift of being a channel for God's healing, and even healers who don't consider any God to be part of their healing would acknowledge that they are a channel for a power rather than being themselves the source of the healing.

There are many healers in Ireland today using different methods from folklore. Most have particular cures for particular maladies such as warts or thrush or ringworm. Most rural communities know of at least one healer in the area, and these healers go about their work quietly over the years. No Irish healer has ever captured the imagination as spectacularly as Finbarr Nolan.

It all started one day in 1970. Finbarr Nolan, seventeen years old, was returning on the school bus to his tiny Cavan hometown of Gowna but the way was jammed by an incredible block of traffic and crowds. The boy walked through the crowd mystified, only to discover that these people had come for one reason only – to be touched by his healing hand. An item on a television programme had told the nation of his many cures. He was a seventh son, and from his infancy people had been healed by him. In the wake of media coverage, the quiet country teenager became a national folk celebrity. As his cures extended beyond the traditionally accepted limits of the seventh son's powers, it was acknowledged that his father had also been a seventh son and so Finbarr was presented in the media as being that rarest of healers – the seventh son of a seventh son.

In the many years since his discovery by the media and the Irish people, Finbarr has experienced highs and lows in his own life and has been the object of both cynicism and adulation. His early fame and wealth might have been his downfall. The carping sceptics might have disheartened him. Instead, he has proven himself to be an admirable survivor.

Through all the exploits the cures have continued, and his gift of healing has been documented and confirmed around the world. Through it all, he has maintained an honest and simple approach to his work. Even though he didn't choose his gift, he knows that it works. Dealing year after year with the sick and hopeless has been a depressing burden which Finbarr has coped with in the realisation that his career was decided the day he was born.

At first, some dismissed him as a faith-healer – that people were cured because they wanted to be or because their ailments were imaginary. But this is disproved by the fact that he has cured animals, infants and cynics alike. Those few who might accuse him of being a fraud are quickly silenced by the weight of evidence supporting his gift and by the unassuming sincerity of the man himself.

In the early days, Finbarr's gift was draped in the legend and religious ritual from which faith in him had sprung. But as he matured and learned more about the healing, he shed the mystique to present himself for what he is – an ordinary man with an extraordinary gift. That gift has decided how he will make a living, but he has never tried to capitalise on it by nurturing ideas of cult or reverence.

The people attending Finbarr's clinics are told plainly that on average half the patients he treats gain significant relief or are fully healed. Given the fact that most who come to him have had no cure from conventional medicine this is a remarkable average. Finbarr states clearly that he has no control over how the healing works. The people come to him three times and he lays his right hand on the bare skin of the affected area.

Finbarr's clinics are quiet and simple. He travels around, working from hotel rooms, treating the many people who come with their various ailments. Those treated by him say he is a calming person, and his approach to his work is methodical and friendly. Finbarr says he is not conscious of doing or trying to do anything when he is treating someone, and the only slightly unusual mannerism I have noticed is that he will touch the affected area with his right hand, then cup his hand, then touch it again. Whatever the many unanswered questions about his healing, the results speak for themselves because the cures, when they happen, are definite and often staggering.

Arthritis, psoriasis, even blindness have been healed. People have been restored from their death-bed to normal working life. Long-endured ailments have disappeared. Cases have been documented and publicised. He is a travelling healer for whom the cures have become almost unremarkable – he records them mainly to quell the cynics. He has never shied away from scrutiny, and regrets the fact that more hasn't been done to investigate his gift.

This quiet, happily married family man has lived through his own naïve excesses and the attempts by others to exploit him. He maintains a regular work pattern nowadays, mostly between Ireland, England and Scotland. Indeed, he is now often invited to professional seminars where people from all walks of life – including doctors – come to learn about healing. In these days of recognising the validity of alternative medicine, Finbarr doesn't face so much of the old scepticism. In the recent past, four doctors have come to him for treatment.

This book is primarily the story of Finbarr's life so far. He has candidly revealed his strengths and weaknesses. There were no precedents for his life: no experienced healer who could advise him about developing his gift; no other country lad who could advise him on sudden wealth; no one in his Cavan hometown to explain how to deal with becoming a focus for national and international media attention. Finbarr doesn't try to hide the mistakes he made. I think he's to be congratulated for that, and for maintaining his honesty and even his sanity through it all.

What follows is Finbarr's own story told in his own words. The book concludes with accounts of ten cures, and two studies carried out on Finbarr and his healing gift.

Martin Duffy,
February 1992

INTRODUCTION

So many things have happened in my life. I was born with
a gift to heal, but I wasn't born perfect. I was affected by
sudden wealth and fame in the same way any ordinary country
lad would be. I was prone to a wanderlust and a naïveté that
led me into many bizarre situations. I have come into conflict
with the media, the Church, and the law. I can't say that I
always feel glad that I was born with my gift, but I think the
life it shaped for me is a story worth telling.

I have never tried to hide the truth from myself or from
others. I've never tried to present myself as being in control
of the healing or as being the best person to be granted such
a gift. Being the seventh son of a seventh son is presumably
something that will become increasingly unlikely as family
size trends change. I suppose that makes me as much a part of

Irish folklore as the legend which set me apart at birth. My book is the story of the cures and the adventures that stemmed from my curious birthright.

The most galling question anyone can ask me is if I've ever cured anyone. It's hardly within the bounds of sense for anyone to imagine that I could have worked full-time as a healer since the age of seventeen without healing people. Maybe the reason such a question arises is that a lot of people don't understand the truth about me or don't comprehend the full story of what my gift has done for others. This book is an attempt to change that.

First and foremost, though, this book is my life story. I didn't choose to be a healer, and I didn't choose to be the focus of so much media attention from such an early age. My fate has shaped my life, and I have done my best to cope with the challenges life presented to me.

People are born with different talents, and it's up to them to use those talents in their lives. If someone was born with a special gift as a football player, it wouldn't make sense for him to hide away and hope that one day he'd be discovered. I feel the same way about my healing powers. I was born with these powers and they were developed in me in a very natural way down the years. I believe I have very strong healing powers, and I want this gift to be used as much as possible. The only way I can do that is by publicising myself and letting people know what I can do. If my talent is left unused those who might benefit from it may never get a chance of being cured. So I like to put across as much positive proof of what I do as I possibly can. It's up to people after that if they want to come to me or not.

My work is often frowned on, yet it is my life. I face scepticism all the time, and I've had to learn to live with that. My attitude now is very simple – I've been healing since I was two years old, I've been doing my work full-time since I was seventeen, and I've seen the results. It doesn't matter if those results don't fit in with the preconceptions of sceptics or the conventional wisdom of the medical profession. I've satisfied myself that there are many thousands of people out there who have been healed by me. I have kept my own file of cases, and anyone who wishes to may see them.

There have often been days when up to fifty people have come to my clinics to tell me they've been cured – the cures might date back to more than twenty years ago. In all the years of journalists investigating me, there has never been any disputing the fact that the cures are there.

On the one hand, I hear people saying that they'd never believe in what I do because it's all nonsense. Then on the other hand, I hear people claiming that what I do works because people are duped by their faith in me. I've never heard of any doctor encouraging a patient to believe in positive vibes and to come off medication. Yet a favourite way of dismissing my results is to say "Ah well, if you believe in this stuff, these things happen".

The majority of doctors are cynical about what I do, despite my results. What they forget is that virtually everybody who comes to me is a medical failure. Most people have consulted a doctor and tried the prescribed treatments before coming to my clinic. People who have been told by their doctor that they have to live with their complaint come to me and many are cured. While I have never claimed to be able to heal everyone or to be the only form of healing, doctors constantly claim that their cure is the only cure.

An interviewer once said to me that if people can't see it, feel it or hear it, they won't believe it. I suppose that's true, but the cynicism about what I do runs much deeper. I have proof of my healing gift, yet many people still refuse to believe.

Part of the problem, I've always believed, is that I have never encouraged any pretence about myself. I am who I am. I think I come across as fairly average and normal. I don't try to contrive any mystery about myself and I don't require people to in some way idolise me if they are to be healed.

I live my life normally and I don't see myself as any different from anyone else. This has created problems – friends of mine find it very hard to understand how I can be something as curious as a healer, and those who see me think that I'm just too ordinary to do the extraordinary things that happen when I heal.

I heal with my right hand. When I'm treating people I don't feel anything – but then, I don't know what I'm supposed to feel. I've been healing all my life. Remembering the first time I healed would be like trying to remember the first time I walked. If, for instance, I'd discovered ten years ago that I could heal then I might be able to recognise the feeling. But the way I heal now is completely natural to me. The only definite trend I have noticed is that a lot of people at my clinics say my hands are very hot. I might treat one person who says my hands are very hot, and then the next person might say my hands don't feel in any way unusual. I'm inclined now to believe that those who feel heat in my hand are being affected by my healing power, although the results don't always confirm this and I have never methodically tried to establish a link between that sensation and a successful cure.

Asthma, arthritis, back ailments and migraine are common complaints that I can heal. At the end of the day, however, it can depend on the individual person. If they respond to the healing gift they'll be cured no matter what the illness. If there is no response, nothing I can do will prevent failure.

A lot of people say to me "You get it so easy, you do nothing for a living". But the work I do is incredibly sad. It's heartbreaking to see a young child terminally ill with cancer, or a young person seriously ill. I want to cure them – I want to cure everybody – but I can't predict anything and so I see the hope people have and the pain they're going through and I do what I do not knowing if I'll be of any help. I have the ability – and I don't know where it comes from – to put all this misery out of my head. It may be part of the gift. I know that if I couldn't deal with the suffering I come in contact with I couldn't carry on as a healer.

While there are no longer any religious references in the way I treat people, I still acknowledge the fact that my healing doesn't come from me and must come from God. Yet coming in contact with so much pain and suffering has led me many times to question the existence of God. I would be happy if there was no such thing as illness and pain to be cured, but that's not the way of life and so I carry on with my work hoping that my healing will help people.

My work earns me enough money to live comfortably, and it has certainly granted me many unusual adventures. That said, the only way people will come to me is if they know that my healing can work. For that reason, I ask people I have cured to allow their stories to be used for publicity. People don't always agree and that's perfectly acceptable. In the final section of this book, though, I have included the stories of ten people I cured down the years. In the course of the book, you will read of many other cures and incidents.

I can't say I'm proud of everything I've done, but I'll leave you to be the judge of how I have used the extraordinary gift I was granted.

ONE

Gowna is a sleepy Cavan village on the main road to nowhere in the heart of Ireland's north midlands. It's a very quiet, quaint place, ideal for a holiday. When I was growing up no one ever locked their doors and the town was very peaceful. The people were friendly and the community was a very close-knit one. But it wasn't a place to live a life. Unemployment was the curse of the town and once you finished school you had to leave to get a job. That was the case for all my brothers.

My father, Bernard, was the local police sergeant. He was a Galway man, the youngest and the seventh son in a family of thirteen, and he settled in Gowna when he married. His father, Patrick Nolan, was a farmer in Ballygar and was known as "the doctor", though my father didn't know why.

My mother, Maureen, came from Donegal. She married my father when she was seventeen and he was thirty. As the years passed they had six children – all boys. There was Patrick, Charles, Bernard, Brendan, Martin, and Sylvester. My father was fifty and my mother thirty-seven when a seventh child was expected. As they already had six sons, there was much speculation among their family and friends as to whether or not the next child would be a boy.

The doctor attending my mother told her he was sure she'd have a boy, and my mother tells me that when I was born, on 2 October 1952, he said, "He'll cure people the way I do."

Within the family it was recognised that I was the seventh son of a seventh son, though I was only known locally as a seventh son. Our family was of average size for the place and time, but we were born into very limiting circumstances. In a place as small as Gowna children were raised to leave because there was little work and no opportunities. There was little future for anyone aside from the eldest of farmers' families in the community, and many of my brothers grew up to follow my father's footsteps into the Gardaí. When I was two years old, my brother Charlie emigrated to America. We had what was known then as an American wake because, at that time, once someone emigrated they would be parted from the family for many years. I only saw Charlie again when I was fourteen. I remember being told what he looked like and being shown photographs of him, and we hired a minibus and drove to Dublin Airport to meet him. I was going to meet a brother I hadn't met before. He has remained a brother really in name alone.

My mother had fantastic hands. You could put a blanket in front of her and she'd make a suit out of it. She was always knitting and embroidering, and as a child I remember her as being forever busy around the house. She was very religious and very family-oriented. She was also a pianist, and was a member of the local amateur dramatic society. My father was a real country fellow. He was very quiet and shy, only coming out of himself when he had a few drinks.

They were kind parents. I don't ever remember getting a slap from them. I only look back on those days at home with fond memories. My parents were well liked and respected in the community – my father because he was a lenient Garda and an amiable man, and my mother because she was a pianist and was very involved with community activities.

As soon as I was born people started coming to the house. I was only two days old when a woman brought her son to me. He was suffering from a painful rash called ringworm. This is a common ailment among country folk since it is passed on to humans mainly through cattle. Folklore has it that the touch of a seventh son is guaranteed to cure ringworm. My mother, however, sent the woman and her son away, saying that there was no way she could allow the hand of her newborn child to be placed on such a contagious disease. The woman insisted that since I was a seventh son I had healing powers, and that it was wrong not to let that power be used. In the days that followed more people came but my mother sent them all away. Her concern for my well-being overruled any talk of a legend.

It was only a matter of time, however, before my mother yielded to the constant flow of demands from local people. One day, a farmer named Hartin came to my mother. He lived just outside the village, and his four-year-old grandson, PJ, had ringworm. He instructed my mother as to what folklore said I should do. To treat ringworm, he said, she had to dip my right hand in holy water and make the sign of the cross with my fingers on the affected area. Then a circle had to be drawn around the infection with my thumb. This, he said, would stop the infection from spreading. Then my hand should be placed on the rash.

Reluctantly, my mother agreed to this. Because she'd been under so much pressure from people about my gift, she felt this would at least be a way of dismissing the rumours if the test failed. She had in her mind that if it worked, she'd accept the fact that I was gifted whereas if it didn't work she could turn people away without feeling guilty.

I was taken out on the back of Hartin's bike to see his boy. The treatment was carried out as prescribed, and I was to go back to see him three times. On the second visit the ringworm had virtually disappeared. On the third it was fully cured.

I was only two and a half years old at the time, and my future had been decided: I was always going to be a healer. From then onwards, when people came to the door suffering from ringworm, my mother would allow them to be treated by me, and I often treated whole families who were infected. In the early days very few came – even so, the seeds had been sown, though I had no idea as a youngster what it all meant.

I remember as a child being brought to treat a horse which had very severe ringworm – his belly was a vast stretch of scabs. I was so small that I had to be lifted up to touch him, yet a few days later all the scabs fell away in a sheet on the field. Some local told my mother, however, that part of the legend was that my healing powers should be used only on humans, and so she became very reluctant to have me treat animals. But when I was a youngster the local farmers used to come along behind my mother's back and take me out to their farms and get me to treat any cattle that had ringworm. They paid me money – which I wasn't supposed to take, but which I was glad to have for sweets.

Gowna was a great place to be very young. There was a lot of freedom around the countryside, and there was never any crime or violence. I enjoyed my freedom and, being the youngest, I was also indulged more than the others. When I was a young child I was very mischievous and I remember a woman complaining to my mother after I'd stolen apples from her orchard. "Mrs Nolan," she said, "you reared six good boys, but I'm afraid this one's a blaggard."

I was a bit spoilt as a child. My father certainly spoiled me a little, and I remember that anything I ever did was blamed on my next-eldest brother, Sylvester. If a rumpus started, there'd be a roar at Sylvester to "leave the child alone", and I'd get away with everything.

The most dangerous adventure I ever went on was as a young boy with two pals. Loch Gowna was frozen over one Christmas, and we three walked the six-mile stretch of the lake. Even now when I think of it I shake at what a risk we were taking.

My mother used to play the organ in the church, and she organised the Altar Society – arranging for women to come in and provide flowers for the church. As a result the parish priest, Canon Kiernan, knew her well. In school they had a catechism test, and if you were good at your catechism you won a little certificate. I was never very good in school, yet I won a certificate. My friends said I'd won it because my mother was such a good friend of the priest – which was probably the truth!

I loved playing football. All I could think of when I got home from school was to get out with my friends and play. As a boy, when we were out playing football, I was always sent to retrieve the ball if it went into a field where cows might have been scratching themselves against the trees. This was a sign they were suffering from ringworm, and as it is so contagious, it is quite possible for people to contract the disease by touching the tree. It was believed I was immune from ringworm – and, indeed, I never caught the disease despite all my contact with it.

Part of the seventh son legend was that to prove your healing power, a worm had to die when placed in your hand. When I was in school this was done several times – as much for amusement as anything else. Most of the time the worm died, but I never liked doing it. The little bit of tourist trade that came to Gowna came because of the fresh-water fishing in the area – the town is almost totally surrounded by lakes. A lot of English tourists would come, and a way for the local lads to earn a little money was to sell worms to the fishermen. My gift, however, prevented me from joining in that enterprise because any worms I touched would die.

One English tourist heard about me and visited our house. He knew all about the legend of the seventh son of a seventh son. He said that a mark of the birthright was for the boy to have seven cures of different ailments. He said that my healing powers extended beyond ringworm, even though that had never been tested. This man told my mother that she would have been able to decide what gift I would have in life by whispering her choice into my ear at birth. She could have chosen one of seven gifts, be it a healer or a fortune-teller or whatever. This presented, for the first time, the idea that I should try to heal other illnesses and when I was eight years old I made my first attempt to treat a disease other than ringworm. A local hotel owner, a returned emigrant from America, had been in a car accident and his arm had been paralysed. This man insisted that I treat him and, when I did, his arm got better. When I look back now, I feel that the cure might not have been genuine – I suspect his arm would have recovered anyway. But the man nevertheless insisted that I had cured him.

This man's father-in-law had rheumatoid arthritis, and I was brought to a town about ten miles away to treat him. He too was cured, and word started to spread that my healing powers were able to deal with all ailments.

The cures still made no great impression on me. I was a child and I paid scant attention to the fact that people were coming to be cured by my gift. Often I'd be in the middle of a football game and I'd be told that someone had arrived for the cure and so I'd go and see them. If it was late in the evening, though, I'd look up at the sun and say, "The sun is set now, I can't do it," and I'd be able to get back to playing football. It was accepted that my power wouldn't work that late in the day.

In those days I was seeing only three or four people a week – and almost all for the treatment of ringworm alone. As ringworm flourished in the early spring and died out by the end of summer, the healing made little impact on my routine. It was very much a local matter and I was just one of many people throughout Ireland who were known in their community to have a healing gift.

But word continued to spread slowly about me in the area. As I got older more people came. There was one doctor who would send anyone with ringworm to me. It became routine for me to come home from school on Mondays and Thursdays and find a few people waiting to be treated by me. At the age of thirteen, though, I didn't see my being the seventh son of a seventh son as anything significant in my life. It was a tradition of the legend that people didn't pay me, so they'd leave gifts of sweets or clothes or a few pence. It seemed to me then that my future would be a matter of getting through school and then leaving Gowna to find work and make a living. I didn't see myself as being different from the rest of the family, and certainly never imagined making a living as a healer.

When I was fourteen, I went to Dublin during the school summer holiday. It was expected that after I'd finished school I'd end up having to go to Dublin or London to find work anyway, and this trip was a kind of preparation for that. I had two brothers working in Dublin at the time and I stayed with them. I worked in a shoe-shop in Mary Street and for the first time I was earning a wage. Even though I was to develop a strong wanderlust in later years, I felt very homesick for Gowna. I became more and more unhappy, and after a month I left Dublin.

In Gowna there was a man named Mickey Smith who owned a drapery shop and also managed a showband called the Hi-Lows. I got a job with him, and carried on working for him part-time after going back to school. I'd work in the shop and would also help out with odd jobs like packing the suits for the band members, polishing their shoes, and loading the wagon for going on the road. That was the nearest I came to an ordinary job and I loved the responsibility and the fact that I had something to do with a showband. I was paid £2.50 a week, which was a great deal of money, and I became more and more enthralled by the world of the bands. They were all the rage then, and my hobby as a young teenager was to follow the showbands at local dances and collect their publicity photos: at one stage I had about four hundred photos of them. It was my love of showbands that started me off on fashionable clothes, since their members always wore the smartest suits in the latest styles and, for me, smart clothes were a part of being grown-up and sophisticated.

By the following summer my next-eldest brother Sylvie was in the Gardai and he was stationed in Fitzgibbon Street station in Dublin. I visited him briefly and while I was there another Garda in the station, Brian Connaughton, was entering for the major cycling race, the Ras Tailtean. Sylvie and I went with Brian down to O'Connell Street for the start of the race, and Brian asked me to wheel the bike along for him as he carried his kit. He set off and in the end he won the race – to the surprise of many who felt he was an outsider. It's said that a seventh son is lucky, and I thought maybe some luck had run off me for him.

By the time I'd reached my early teens, about nine or ten people were coming to me a week. The gift was still very tightly restricted – Mondays and Thursdays, between the hours of sunrise and sunset. If people came on a Tuesday, for example, they were sent away. This was part of the legend, and it was many years before I questioned that.

My way of treating people was very religious. I would make the sign of the cross on the affected area with holy water saying, "In the name of the Father, and of the Son, and of the Holy Ghost, amen, amen, amen, amen . . ." and I'd touch the affected part again and again with my right hand.

Gowna was a mainly Catholic town, with just a handful of Protestants. I remember once a Protestant man came to me with ringworm. I had to treat him as I treated all others – with the holy water and prayer. We felt embarrassed about treating this man, afraid he'd be offended by the religious references. My mother took him aside and explained apologetically about the Catholic content of the treatment, but he took the whole matter straightforwardly. "I don't give two damns what he does – if the Canon could cure me I'd go to him," he said. As it turned out he was cured, and he came back to me in later years with other ailments.

As more people came to me, however, I also became increasingly aware of my failures. If I treated someone and they weren't cured, I'd think at first I'd treated them in the wrong way and I'd try again. In time I had to acknowledge that my healing didn't always work, and my mother and I held the theory that only people who believed in the idea of healers could be healed.

One day, a black cat showed up outside the door and it just wouldn't go away no matter how hard we tried to discourage it. It was so persistent that we finally took it in. My father, being a superstitious man, said this was a sign of good luck to come. Shortly afterwards, I got the phone call which changed my life.

As the cures continued, my mother was spreading the word, telling her friends and relatives about me. My mother is from Donegal, and when I was seventeen she brought me to her sister-in-law there who had arthritis. This turned out to be one of the most significant steps in my life as a healer. When I arrived, there were a hundred people waiting to see me. The word had spread, and they all wanted to be healed. I had never seen so many people together seeking treatment from me, and I was excited to be the centre of so much attention.

There was an old lady there, a friend of my mother, who gave us a place to see the people. I had to see them three times – and this would have to be on either Monday or Thursday so we had to go back and forth for a while. This flurry of people came to the attention of the local newspaper, the *Donegal Democrat*, which ran a small article saying "the seventh son of a seventh son appears in Donegal".

At that time, there was a programme presented by Frank Hall called *Newsbeat* on RTE television. Its format was to present the news from small local papers to the nation – sometimes lampooning, and sometimes taking things seriously. A researcher from the programme saw the item in the newspaper and decided to follow it up.

One evening after the spate of visits to Donegal, I sat at home doing my homework. There was a knock on the door and the postmaster, Jimmy Sloan, stood breathless before us. "Finbarr! Come up quick! Come up to the phone!" He gasped. "RTE are on wanting to talk to you."

A man spoke to me for RTE. He said they'd read about me and wanted to do an item for *Newsbeat*. He asked if I'd have any objections, and of course I said I wouldn't. He set a time and a date for coming to interview me and my family, and then rang off.

When I stepped out into the empty street I jumped into the air and did a dance with delight. I had no sense of business then and no idea of what lay ahead. All I knew was that only famous people were ever on television – John Wayne and Clint Eastwood and Gay Byrne – and now I was about to be on television too. I never dreamed that the publicity would be of any relevance to my life.

When I'd been in Donegal, I had treated a man who ran a small fabric factory and he'd given me a sheet of beautiful green material. As I was going to be on television, I went into Cavan town and had a tailor there make a double-breasted jacket out of the material. Double-breasted jackets with shiny buttons were all the rage then.

When the big day came in March 1970, I was allowed to take the day off school and I waited for the RTE people to arrive. Early in the afternoon, a huge bus pulled into Gowna with the RTE symbol on its side. A crew of six climbed out with their cameras and equipment. It was an impressive sight to have the likes of this in Gowna, and hundreds of people came into the village that evening just to see the camera crew at work.

They interviewed me – wearing my new jacket – sitting beside my mother on an armchair, and they interviewed my father. They were very pleasant and very interested in me. Then they spoke to some local people who had been cured – mostly of ringworm – and filmed me treating people. They also interviewed Father Murphy, the local curate.

Newsbeat were supposed to phone me and let me know when the show was going out. One night, however, we turned on the television and there I was. On the programme there were other seventh sons – one a very young lad, another a farmer. As it turned out they didn't get the same response I got. I believe it was the priest, Father Murphy, who made all the difference. He said that he had taught me in school and that he had brought to me a man on crutches with arthritis and the man was cured and had thrown his crutches away. To have a priest say on Irish television that you had cured someone has a huge effect on people. He said he felt that God's healing could work through people and agreed with the interviewer's opinion that what I did could be described as a miracle.

"I believe Finbarr has faith and the people who come to him have faith," he said, "and I believe that's enough to explain any cures that there are."

The next day in school I was the centre of attention. I was being nicknamed "the film star", and everyone was saying that they'd seen me. There was great joy and elation in the family that the whole thing had gone so well and we were all delighted to have been on television. There were other developments brewing, however, that I could never have imagined.

There were very few phones in the village, and anyone who wanted to contact me had to do so through RTE. Those who enquired were told that I saw people after school on Mondays and Thursdays. I suppose I expected that more people would come to me after the *Newsbeat* item, but I had no idea just how much interest had been aroused around the country. It was still fairly early days for television in Ireland, and the programme had a large audience. This combination meant that I was in for an amazing shock.

I came home from school the next Thursday after the show and there was a huge traffic jam in the town. The bus couldn't get into the village, and I thought there'd been some kind of a disaster. We all stared out of the bus trying to figure out what was going on. We were left off at the crossroads outside the village and I walked through the crowds to my house. I discovered then why the people were there.

"It's him. It's him!" I heard people say. The crowd parted before me as I walked to my home. Everyone looked at me in a kind and loving way. It was then that I realised – all these people had come to see me.

I went into the house in a state of shock and my mother was waiting for me in a frantic state. "Come on! Come on! Eat your dinner quick! All these people have come to see you!"

She gave me a small meal, and then I went into the living-room as people were allowed in a few at a time. The crowds grew outside as I worked. The room would fill, I'd treat them all and they'd leave, and the room would fill again. I carried on, treating people as quickly as I could, and even as the evening set in there were many more outside. It was then that I took my first step outside the traditional beliefs of the legend. I kept on treating people until I'd seen everyone. It was past midnight, and I was stunned and exhausted.

I was too young to even comprehend what was going on. At that time, like any young boy, I had many hobbies. One was that I used to have a note-book in which I kept the names and addresses of people who had come to me over the years. My aim was to eventually have a name from every county in Ireland. The only county I was missing was Waterford. That night, two people came to me from Waterford and I had achieved my ambition.

The next day I was allowed to miss school. The excitement was incredible and the events of the day before were the talk of the area. I had expected a response from being on tele-vision, but nothing like this. To me, the world had never seemed a big enough place to have so many people come to the seventh son of a seventh son. I had never given serious consideration to my gift or to where it might lead. I had never imagined that it could change the path of my life. But I was seventeen years old. There was much more to come that I wouldn't be equipped to handle.

TWO

Looking back, it's like a dream. In a tiny Irish village there was a young healer. The country heard about him, and suddenly flocked to him in their thousands. I find it hard to believe that what happened to me really did happen. I was an ordinary boy going to school, but overnight I was suddenly turned into a national folk celebrity. Thousands of people were coming and there literally weren't enough hours in the day to see them all. I'd get back from school by half past five, and the clinics would continue into the night with throngs of people outside.

One day at the height of the crowds, my father went up to the shops to get food for my dinner. Coming back, he had to make his way through the crowds to the house. He got a belt from the stick of an old man who told him to get back to the

end of the queue. My mother used to say that she was the
only person in the world to know what it was like to have ten
thousand people knock on her door.

Gowna was a very small village with a population of eighty-
eight. There were no main streets. It consisted basically of
three pubs-cum-grocery-shops, a school, a church and little
else. But after the *Newsbeat* item the village was booming.
Thousands flocked to this tiny place, and there were constant
traffic jams. The Gardaí were trying to cope with the traffic,
and every house had its sign up saying "bacon, egg and sau-
sage, tea, bread and butter – three and sixpence". The one
guest-house in the town was packed out from morning till
night, and traders were pleading with me to see people every
day of the week instead of just Mondays and Thursdays so
the crowds might be spread out more manageably.

As for me, I don't know how I coped. There were times in
those early days when I was seeing as many as two and a half
thousand people a day – I couldn't begin to imagine doing it
now. It seemed as if everyone in Ireland who was ill and
couldn't be cured by a doctor was beating a path to my door.
There were people in wheelchairs, people who were terminally
ill, many desperate cases. I'd never dreamt there could be so
much suffering among people, yet it hardly sank in. I just took
each day as it came.

Gallons of holy water would be blessed by the local priest
and it was then carried beside me in a small dish like a sugar
bowl. I'd dip my thumb in the holy water and make the sign
of the cross over the person's ailment. Then I'd place the palm
of my right hand on the ailment. I'd move along through the
people in this way, wondering mostly at the time of how I'd
ever manage to treat everyone who was waiting their turn.

There was a superstition that water touched by a seventh
son could heal. This led to a situation where many people

would take away the holy water I had touched in tablet bottles to use on their ailments – though I never heard of anyone cured that way. Requests were also coming for me to touch cloth that people would use like relics, but we never agreed to do that.

My brother Brendan was a carpenter working in Dublin when the whole pandemonium of my success broke out. He hadn't much work at the time, and he was easily convinced to come back to Gowna, as we badly needed someone to organise the crowds swarming around our home. When Brendan took over the handling of the crowds, his first ingenious move was to go up the street to workmen who were digging up the road and borrow some barrels and planks from them. He set up a system using four barrels and three planks across them like a turnstile. People were allowed in and out of the house in an orderly fashion. My routine was to see about fifteen people in the house at a time, and Brendan became the man who would stand by the plank and allow each group to come and go in turn. This plan didn't always work out right, however, because people realised there was a lane to the back door and they would queue there as well. My mother, being soft-hearted, would let these people in also and I'd end up with a crowd in the living-room.

We tried at one time to give people tickets to see me. We bought the books of tickets locally, but some villagers bought the same tickets and would come back and sell them to people in the queue so that I'd end up with ten people in a room all with the same ticket number. The only solution was to control the queue.

Brendan would roar and shout at people to get back and stay in line – he was a great organiser, though sometimes gruff. He was not always up to the tricks of the people who wanted to find some short-cut through the long wait to see me, though. One woman went to him saying that her aunt had died and she was anxious to get back. She was allowed to skip the queue and I treated her. Later that evening, she was seen in the pub.

To complicate matters even more, my father was replying to letters from people seeking an appointment with me, and giving these people the impression that they had appointments when in fact he was just letting them know when I started my work on the day they wanted to come to Gowna; the whole thing was chaotic and exhausting. I'd start seeing people after I'd come home from school and had my dinner, and the clinics sometimes went on past midnight. Then I'd fall into bed.

The Nolans became famous in the area, and my father would be treated to drink after drink in the local pub by people who recognised him. The excitement around me was tremendous, and my mother was on cloud nine over people coming to her and marvelling at her young son. My mother looked on the whole affair from a religious point of view. She was delighted to see so many people being cured through me, and she felt that I had been chosen by God to heal people. While the crowds waited to see me, they would say the rosary outside our house. I didn't particularly approve of all the religious references – I felt that such things should be confined to greater things than my gift.

The fact that I'd been on television and that people were thronging to me went completely to my head. I felt wanted and it was a great sensation. People needed me, and they were gloating over me, and they were getting cured. I was a very naïve country boy, not particularly good at school, and full of my own preoccupations about football and showbands. At least nobody could accuse me of being a cheat – I was so obviously innocent. People would look at me and say I was sent from God. I was an awkward boy at the centre of a whirlpool.

One of the superstitions about the healing was that if you take money you lose the power, and so I didn't suggest any donations until much later on in my life – I started taking money only when I finally realised that healing was going to become my livelihood. Money was coming in, though, and people were giving me little gifts.

Shortly after the *Newsbeat* item the family thought that the whole thing would die out in a matter of weeks. But then the national newspapers became interested in the story too, and they created a new surge of interest. It was referred to as the "mini-Lourdes", and the crowds swelled even more. The village was bursting at the seams with people coming. It just couldn't cope – there were traffic jams for miles around.

The first sour note in all the excitement occurred, ironically, by the very same way I was first introduced to the nation. The *Newsbeat* team returned six weeks later to do a follow-up story on my success, since they had first set the whole thing in motion. On that first visit they had been polite and enthusiastic. When they returned, however, they were cynical and spent all their time emphasising the money and the disorganisation. The interviewer had won my confidence from the first item and I told him, in naïve confidence, that I'd earned a thousand pounds. When the item was transmitted, he included my comment in his report. There were interviews with people talking about their long hours waiting to see me and about the chaos in the town. People were being asked how much they were giving me, though no one cared to talk about such things because of the superstition about giving anything to a healer.

I was interviewed walking down the traffic-filled street. The interviewer commented on my new red suit and asked me if

I still felt I was healing people if I had to rush them through in groups instead of dealing with them one by one. I was exhausted at the time and under a lot of pressure. "I have no peace at all," I said. "Every day of the week there's people calling to me. I'm just fed up making cures but I have to see them. I don't think I'll stick it. I don't think I'll make my livelihood out of it."

I met the interviewer many years later in a night-club and said hello to him. "Are you still conning people?" he asked. I got very angry – it almost came to blows.

The second *Newsbeat* item was shown in May, and I was supposed to be studying for my Inter Cert. The crowds were so big and the confusion so great that it was agreed I could leave school and not return until after the summer holidays at which point I'd go back a year in class. It was expected that by then the whole thing would have blown over. All this excitement around me felt like the high point of my life, and the thought of going back to school after suddenly achieving this kind of fame and fortune was dreadful. I knew in my heart and soul that I didn't want to go back to school. I had no interest in education and, with all the excitement, I couldn't keep my head in a school book. It was like someone being in jail, and then being let out, and yet told that he has to go back in soon. That's how I felt about school. As it turned out, I never returned to my studies. Healing became my full-time career – my life – and I had to make the best of it. The sixth brother of the family, Sylvester, always used to joke about how unfair God had been to him by making him the one short of fame and fortune. He didn't realise the full story of what was happening to me.

As the people continued flooding in, we realised that it was simply impossible to deal with them in my house. The only place nearby that seemed possible to use was an old shell of a school down the road, and I moved in there even though it was filthy and disused. It was the only way I could deal with the crowds coming to me. The parish priest gave the keys to the building gladly – he even offered us the use of the church, but my mother declined because she felt the church would be destroyed with all the crowds passing through.

From this new base, it became easier to deal with the crowds. People came in a few hundred at a time, in separate groups of women and men, and I would treat them all in turn. Brendan would gather contributions, and at the end of the treatment of each group we would all say a few prayers before those people left and the next group filed in. The crowds kept coming, and my reputation continued to spread.

Initially, there was a string of reporters coming to interview me in Gowna. One day a woman came from a magazine. She talked very pleasantly to me, but then she went away and wrote what I could only describe as a hatchet job. She described me as being bandy-legged, and she portrayed the local priest as a gruff, grey old man. She also went to the editor of a local paper who had nothing complimentary to say about me either. When the article appeared my parents were ashamed and upset. My father was so annoyed he said there would be no more interviews done. He turned many away, but then a man who wrote for the *Sunday Press* came to Gowna.

I was completely taken in by him – he was a real charmer and made such a good impression on my parents that an interview was agreed. He spoke to many people who had been cured, and the photographer who accompanied him took a picture of a man pushing his wheelchair out of a clinic. A full-page report entitled "The amazing cures of Finbarr Nolan" appeared on the back of the *Sunday Press*, swelling the crowds coming to me.

The national press made a lot of my use of holy water, and in the face of such criticism I eventually decided to stop using it. Rural Irish people accepted the use of holy water, but for people who weren't Roman Catholics, and for the urban readership of the papers, the holy water was not in good taste. It made me uncomfortable and it made them uncomfortable. I feared at first that not using the holy water would make a difference, but in fact it didn't.

Brendan's belief in me was total. He would often get angry when someone was not cured. He would come up with all kinds of reasons to try to explain the failures. But the cures were almost secondary at the time. People would come to me saying they'd been in a wheelchair before being treated by me but were now able to walk. I was so busy trying to keep up with the crowds that I'd barely acknowledge them. I didn't take names and addresses then, as I do now. It was just mass disorganisation. The job as I saw it was to get the people in, treat them, move them on and get the next crowd in.

With the kind of adaptability that comes from being young and blissfully ignorant, I was more interested in getting on with enjoying my life than in keeping count of the people whose lives I had changed. My own teenage whims were never far from the surface either. One time, a member of Big Tom's backing band, the Mainliners, came to Gowna with his mother to have her treated by me. He waited and waited in the queues, but then had to leave to get to a gig on time. When he came next time, he saw me while I was out taking a break. He called me aside and asked me if there'd be any chance that I might see his mother. When he told me he was with the Mainliners, I set all aside. Showbands were still my main obsession in life, and I was delighted to meet a member of one of the most popular bands of the day. His mother was brought in and given VIP treatment, and in return he gave me his autograph on a photo of the Mainliners. He also told me to go to the dance the following night in Carrigallen and

I'd be introduced to Big Tom. I did, and it was a great thrill to be allowed backstage to meet one of my heroes – for me, it was like meeting the president. I was delighted to meet Big Tom, and we chatted away about our being in the Irish limelight.

As the crowds continued, a journalist came from the *Sunday People* and asked the usual questions. The following week the paper's headline was "Bishop probes Finbarr's miracles". Bishop Daly of Ardagh and Clonmacnoise, who has since become a cardinal, had heard about me. He was quoted as saying, "I heard about the goings-on at Gowna and I'm very concerned about it. I think he's using religion for superstitious ends, and I don't approve of it."

I thought that was the finish of it and that I'd be back to school next week. All the Irish papers took up the story, and it was on front pages the following Monday. I believed the crowds would die off. I thought that with Ireland being so Catholic, the bishop's opinions would stop people from coming. Instead, the whole thing ignited completely. Thousands more flooded in. It even became a matter of curiosity, with people coming from miles away just to see the crowds.

Shortly afterwards the parish priest, for many years a friend of my mother, came into the house. Even though there were a thousand people waiting to see me, he said he had to halt my use of the school hall immediately. No amount of pleading from us could change his mind, and he left with the keys. Brendan was furious with him, but there was nothing we could do. I was left stranded with no facilities in the village for the crowds outside.

The only place I could take them was to an old warehouse where cement used to be stored. I went down and worked there for a few hours, and the place was packed with people in wheelchairs and on crutches. The dust was rising and people were dirtying their clothes. I couldn't bear the idea of them having to put up with such squalor; I couldn't have people coming from all over Ireland and then being treated by me in such a place.

In exasperation, I walked out and got into Brendan's car. I was determined to find somewhere decent from which to work. We went four miles down the road to a place called Colmcille. I spoke to the owner of the local dance-hall there, and arranged with him to use his hall. It could hold six hundred people, so the crowds would be dealt with properly.

It was sad to move out of Gowna. It was a very poor place and it had been experiencing its first ever boom. But I had to go back there and lead the procession of cars out of the town to my new base. Five hundred cars pulled out of the town behind me on the road to Colmcille. Gowna had gone from being a sleepy village to being a bustling town. As the cars drove away, the village went back to sleep. The traders and business-people blamed the priest, and even went so far as seeking the intervention of Cardinal Dalton. But I never worked from Gowna again.

There was a sand quarry half a mile down the road from the hall I was using in Colmcille. Every Monday and Thursday, when I held my clinics, it had to close because its lorries couldn't get past the jam of cars parked on both sides of the narrow roads around the hall. The Gardaí came and put pressure on me because they couldn't cope with the crowds and the traffic. I sympathised with them even though they were forever moving me on. I'm sure they had chosen their quiet country stations to suit their lives, and then along I'd come with thousands of patients, their friends, and the onlookers. Chaos followed me everywhere.

During that time there was a tragic incident which sparked a swipe at me from a local paper called the *Longford News*.

The *Longford Leader* was the upmarket paper for the area, while the *Longford News* was much like a tabloid. The owner of the paper was a man named Vincent Gill, and he ran a column called "Pilgrim's Progress" in which he often mentioned me. On one particular occasion, he ran a sarcastic item titled "Miraculous Cure at Faith Healer's Clinic". The story went on to tell of a man who had suffered greatly with arthritis but hadn't had any pain since coming to the clinic – because he was dead.

The man had come to me from Northern Ireland. At that stage in the clinics I'd see women first, and the hall would be packed – perhaps six or seven hundred people there. I also used to pray over the assembled crowd after I'd touched each person – I'd say an Our Father, a Hail Mary, and a Glory Be. Usually, everyone stayed until I'd dealt with the last person and said my prayers. Then the doors would open and there would be a throng of people rushing out as those outside would bustle to come in for their turn. This Northern Ireland man was caught between the two crowds and he died. The papers reported the incident and the health authorities came down and made new regulations about crowd-control and fire escapes and so on.

By now, though, deputations were coming to me from every town around asking me to set up clinics there. They would come offering plans for managing the traffic, details about the facilities available for the people who'd come to see me, and free use of a hall. So much business was generated around me that it was worthwhile for any town to have me use it as a base.

I went to a town called Arvagh, which was four miles from both Colmcille and Gowna. Arvagh was a small town with a population of about five hundred people. I used the parish hall there, which was very big and could easily hold eight hundred people. Everything was going fine, the hall was constantly packed out, and the controversy was boosting crowds rather than reducing them. The end of the town where I was based was doing a huge amount of business.

But one day the bishop of that diocese – Bishop Quinn – demanded that I stop using the hall. A deputation from the town went to the bishop to appeal, and he finally agreed to give me two weeks' notice to leave. I was on the move again.

This time, though, I decided to move just down the road. There was an old cinema named the Moonlight Pavilion at the bottom of the town, and I bought it for six hundred pounds. The figure was extremely low, but the town committee coaxed the owners so that I'd stay in the area. A lot of painting and renovation was needed on the cinema, and the local people teamed together to get the work done at a reasonable cost. I set up the clinic there and the crowds followed. The Moonlight Pavilion became my permanent base, and I would work there without interference for nearly two years.

After my troubles with the bishops I put less and less emphasis on religion in the way I treated people and I personally lost my faith to a certain extent. As I watched people getting relief or being healed completely, I couldn't see anything wrong in what I was doing and I couldn't see why the bishops had attacked me. I started to reduce the religious references and stopped saying prayers over people until finally there was no religious content left in my healing. I had noticed, also, that about half the cars around my clinics had Northern Ireland registrations and I was concerned that Catholic references in my healing would offend people of other religions.

In a very short space of time I had become established as a celebrity and there was constant curiosity about me. Up to the time when people around the country learned of me and my gift, the lakes were the only thing that drew outsiders to Gowna. Tour buses would come through the village during the summer full of Americans and English people on the way to these beauty spots. Our home became a new stop on the tour, however, and sometimes the drivers would knock on the door and ask me to come out to pose for photographs for the tourists.

With Arvagh as my base, I worked methodically at my routine, still healing only on Mondays and Thursdays. It's actually only in recent years that I've heard many of the stories of the cures from the early days in Gowna. The need to organise proof or money, the need to figure out how all this would affect my life – none of this dawned on me for a long time. Within a matter of months I'd gone from being a schoolboy with a part-time job in the local hardware store to being a national figure – with one element above all in my life that I didn't know how to cope with: money.

THREE

Despite the success and the floods of people, my behaviour remained ordinary for a lad of my age. I loved going to dances, and I loved chasing girls and messing around with my pals. People would look at me and say, "Is that Finbarr Nolan? It couldn't be." But then again, ignorance is bliss. Because I was so naïve about the whole thing, I never fully felt the pressure that was on me as the focus of so much attention. Most of the time, I hardly even realised that I was a healer or that Finbarr Nolan was a famous name in Ireland.

I was just a kid, out playing football on the street with my friends. I was no different from anybody else, but the publicity started making people see me differently. It was amazing the way the attitudes of the local people changed towards me. After the publicity, they were almost afraid to talk to me. They would stand back from me, staring silently. A lot of people in the area became sceptical and maybe even jealous when they saw just how successful I'd become. I started getting poison-pen letters. My parents wouldn't let me read them, and they took them to the Gardaí. The Gardaí had some suspicions which they followed up but nothing ever came of it. However, the letters stopped after a while.

When the publicity and the crowds were huge, a reporter arrived in Gowna looking for me. She stopped a local man to ask where I lived and he gave her directions. Then he added, "But he won't talk to you – he's gone independent now."

When I was seventeen I had a stack of money, and I wanted a car. I had to wait until I was eighteen to realise my dreams, but I got a provisional licence and bought a brand-new, red Renault 1300. I ordered the car but I couldn't drive it – I had to wait six months to come of age. When the car was delivered, its registration number turned out to be NID 777. My mother insisted that the car be blessed, and Father Murphy did so. It was all over the papers that I owned a car, and, of course, there was great emphasis on the number. People phoned up the county council office wanting to find out if I'd specially ordered the number plates.

In the end I had to get rid of the car. Life became unbearable because no matter where I went I was recognised. People would blow their horns or shout after me on the streets. I'd be stopped as I drove along by people asking if there was any chance of my following them up the road to see a relative.

My next car was an Audi which wasn't as conspicuous and after that I changed cars regularly. I was a child, and cars were my favourite toys. I had no sense in the matter.

As a teenager I loved going to dances and discos. But jokes used to follow me, one being that the women in the discos were chasing me – they wanted to beat me up for taking the stiffness out of the men. I was able to indulge my love of fashion as a teenager too, and whatever the trend was, I followed it. At one stage there was a fad for corduroy boots and flared jeans, which I bought. I wore see-through shirts and I grew my hair long. As soon as I could, I started growing a beard.

Football had always been a great love of mine, but as my fame grew, it became more and more difficult to play with the other lads of my age. People became increasingly removed from me, and also my parents worried that I might injure myself. In the end, I had to give up football.

My response, with so much money suddenly in my hands, was to buy a speedboat. I'd go water-skiing on Loch Gowna, and the locals would come out to watch. One local paper had a report saying "Finbarr Nolan seen walking across the Lakes of Gowna . . . on skis."

Based in the Moonlight Pavilion and with crowds coming to me constantly, I was earning a lot of money. But I had no one to advise me on what to do with it or how to invest it or what to expect in terms of tax. As a young lad in a small village, I was living by a simple code – you didn't tell anyone your private business for fear gossip would be spread about you. So I kept to myself and carried on with my healing work not knowing what to do about my income and my fame.

My story drew the attention of the media everywhere, and even the international Press Association was coming in. When I was eighteen, CBS decided to do a seven-minute item on the seventh son of a seventh son. I was living in Gowna (population eighty-eight), and my story was to be screened across America. I was interviewed by Bob Simons, who later went on to be international news himself when he disappeared during the Gulf War. I was foolish enough at the time to think that nothing I said for American television would ever reach Ireland, and when I was asked how much I'd earned I said forty thousand pounds. The item went out on CBS evening news, and was reported next day in the Irish papers.

The taxman was reading all this, and contacted me. I got a bill for the tax on forty thousand pounds earned between the ages of two and fourteen, and I didn't know what to do with it. I asked a local man who I believed to have some understanding of these things.

"Tell them to fuck off with themselves," was his advice, plain and simple. He said that my income consisted of donations from people and there was no tax on what people willingly gave you as a gift. "You don't charge any money, so you have no income."

I stupidly wrote back to the tax office saying I had no tax to pay. As it happened, at that time donations actually were tax-free. It was only shortly afterwards that a law was passed making donations taxable, and I believe it was because of my case. Obviously, the reply given on the assessment form angered the tax people. They came down on me like a ton of bricks.

My ultimate indulgence proved to be in many ways my downfall. I bought a brand-new Jaguar XJ6 when I was eighteen. I believe I was the youngest person in the world at that time driving around in a Jaguar bought by myself from my own money. Now, I'd also say I was the biggest idiot in the world driving around in such a car. It was sheer stupidity on my part and it ultimately led to my bankruptcy.

There were hundreds of people coming to me and the newspapers, having first concentrated on the cures, started to look at the whole area of money. One paper calculated that I was earning a pound per person. The papers were no longer interested in writing about people healed, or in talking to people cured. They just started creating a whole myth around the money.

"How much are you making?" was their main question to me instead of asking who I had healed.

At that time, people made voluntary donations and, contrary to what most people think, the amount of money I made during those first years wasn't huge. People would say, "This is my first time, I'll pay you on the third." But by the time the third visit came they might leave a pound note. Others would say at the end of the third visit that they paid the first time. Then there were people coming who would give nothing, or perhaps some coins.

There were so many people coming to me then that there was no way of keeping track and we simply had to trust them to donate something; the whole thing was mass confusion. At that time, tin boxes and grocery bags were being passed around for donations. Brendan would move around the people with a bag, almost like a church collection. People would put their hand into the bag, but there was no knowing if any donation was being made. But the newspapers saw it differently. They might stop one person and ask them how much they had given, and on the basis of such answers they'd calculate the money coming to me.

I was interviewed by the *Sunday Press* at about this time, and the interviewer was a very charming man who had a talent for drawing me into saying things that I thought were off the record.

"You must be earning a hundred grand a year," he said. "Ah yeah, yeah," I replied, "no problem."

There was no limit to my naïveté. I was more interested in being friendly than in thinking that this was an interview for a national newspaper. At the time I had my Jaguar, and he had me pose in front of it for a photo to go with the article. Like a child with his favourite toy, I sat proudly on the bonnet with a cigar in my hand and smiled. I'd never even smoked a cigar before. The story appeared, and the headline over it was: "I've earned a hundred thousand pounds". After that, the tax people were out for me. I imagine they went stone mad when they saw that article.

With the tax demands pouring in, I went to an accountant in Dundalk to try to figure out how to handle the situation. I sat down with him in an attempt to sort out my mess – I was expecting the revenue commissioners to believe I wasn't earning anything, while at the same time I was letting the media believe I was earning a fortune. Looking back on it now, my behaviour at the time was very stupid. It was the stupidity of a child – and that's all I was. A child wants the best toy, and the best toy to me then was a Jaguar. All it did in the end was bring attention, resentment and jealousy down on myself. The publicity about money caused bad feeling among the people coming to me and their numbers started falling. The media had brought the crowds to me, but the media was also proving to be my downfall.

The cures continued through all this, even if the media hardly noticed and I wasn't keeping track of them. One man made such a spectacular recovery that he pushed his own wheelchair out of the clinic. I received a letter from him a month or so later explaining that due to his illness he'd had to sell off the livestock on his farm, but he was now fit enough to re-stock it. He asked me if I would send him three thousand pounds to do so.

The clinics started shrinking as the years passed, and the numbers settled over time. By my second year in Arvagh, people came at a rate of three to four hundred a day. It was still a huge number, but I felt that I had been a novelty to people and that the novelty was wearing out. It was time to change things, and I made a move then which took me away from Gowna and Cavan forever.

In the heyday of media coverage about me I was so well known that I was called on to do the kind of things any celebrity would do. I would be invited to open festivals, judge beauty competitions, or even act as disc jockey in discos. On one fateful occasion I was invited to go to Castleisland in Kerry to open a festival. Brendan and I drove the long way south, and when we arrived, I found there were a thousand people there waiting specifically to be treated by me. I was given a marquee to work from, and I stood there for hours – supplied with tea and sandwiches – as the people flowed through. As a cure usually requires three visits, the local committee organising the festival arranged a hall for me to see people on the other two occasions. I ended up holding clinics there for three months.

People had often written asking me to do clinics around the country. Some people were afraid of coming to Arvagh because it was close to Northern Ireland and the troubles there. In the light of that huge response in Castleisland, Brendan and I decided that the best approach to my work would be to become a travelling healer. It was the start of many, many years of moving around the country. We eventually established a routine of choosing an area and setting up clinics, usually spending six weeks there seeing people, and then going on to another area about fifty miles away. It made sense and it meant that people didn't have to travel so far to see me.

The first regular clinic I started was in Balgriffin, in north County Dublin. The clinics were so successful that a special bus service was set up to bring people to me. The location was perfect, because it took in Dublin and many surrounding areas.

Once I made the decision to become a travelling healer, I decided to step outside the legend's limitations of working only on Mondays and Thursdays because it was impractical.

I had already dropped the other elements one by one – the holy water, the prayers, the limitation of sunrise and sunset – and each step made me slightly nervous, but I found that the cures went on. One thing I never changed was the three visits, considered to be in the name of the Father, the Son and the Holy Ghost. The healing always seemed to need that.

In the early days it seemed that no matter where I set up a clinic, at least five or six hundred people would come every day. I remember once holding a clinic in Claremorris and four hundred people showed up one day – I was so disappointed I almost cried. I could only work in ballrooms at that stage, and when we were going to book a ballroom, if the owner said the capacity was less than four hundred we'd have to try somewhere else.

By 1972, most of the family were living in Dublin. My mother's sister was also living there, and I decided to buy my parents a house in Raheny so that the family could be reunited. Myself and two other brothers who were working in Dublin lived in the house with them.

When I moved to Dublin I was asked on to *The Late Late Show*, the most popular programme on Irish television. I was invited to bring along half a dozen people who had been cured. There was a taxi-driver in the Cavan area whom I treated and healed. He later ran a mini-bus service from Monaghan to Gowna, and in order to facilitate him I would treat his passengers as soon as they arrived so that he could make the return journey and bring a new load. He saw many of the passengers cured. I thought this taxi-driver would be a good man to have on the show, as he had been cured himself and had also seen so much. When we phoned him up to ask, he said "Yeah, I'll go on *The Late Late Show*, but you have to pay me a hundred pounds and the show has to pay me a hundred pounds." We refused to bring him on the programme.

Publicity has always been very important to me, and I was anxious about how my appearance before the nation would go. In the end, I felt I didn't come across so well. There were a number of doctors on the show, and Dr John O'Connell – many years later the Minister for Health – was the only one who was in any way positive about my work. There was a woman on *The Late Late Show* whom I'd cured of arthritis. One of the doctors dismissed her completely, and the woman stood up and declared that she had been in intense pain for fifty years with arthritis, saying, "And don't you try to tell me that I wasn't!" She got a big round of applause.

A reporter who had written about me before also appeared on the show. He said he'd gone around Gowna looking for people who hadn't been cured by me and couldn't find any. Yet he made a big deal about the fact that I'd just come back from a holiday in the Bahamas and that I'd earned a hundred thousand pounds one year. Perhaps his problem was that he got to know me well and discovered that I was a normal teenager and he couldn't understand how I could have such a strong healing gift.

Probably the most spectacular cure I ever carried out happened in 1972. A man named William Jackson, who was suffering from multiple sclerosis, came to me from Scotland after seeing an item about me on television. I treated him, and the next morning he was able to get up and walk around the town. It was just incredible to see a man arrive one day in an invalid car and be brought into the clinic in a wheelchair by his wife, and the next day to see him out and about. There was a dinner-dance in the local hotel that night, and he was so full of life he took on the job of doorman.

I contacted a local photographer and reporter to come and record the story, and Jackson was interviewed standing beside his invalid car and talking about his cure. When all this was done, the cured man turned to me and asked how much he'd be paid for the story. I felt very disheartened, and believed it was wrong to pay a man to tell the true story of his cure. In the end, though, I had to agree.

When I decided to venture into Northern Ireland, I was very aware of the dangers of being there. Brendan and I decided to phone the various political parties and organisations to see if they would mind my working in the North. I didn't want to take any chance of becoming a terrorist target or creating any tensions. No one suggested there would be any problems, so I didn't feel so nervous. I opened up a clinic outside Lurgan in Armagh in a tiny village called Aghalee. The inhabitants were Protestant. There was a fine big hall there, and I reckoned it had a good hinterland of towns.

The welcome I got from the local people was marvellous. There was no hotel in the little town, but locals would come to the clinic inviting me to their homes for tea in the evenings. I was very popular and many people were coming to me. There was a Dr Wilson in the village, and while I was there he coincidentally went away on holiday. At that time Harold Wilson was the Prime Minister of Britain. Someone put a sign up on the doctor's door saying, "Wilson out, Finbarr in".

Around that time I appeared on a TV show in Northern Ireland, and they took me into a Belfast hospital a week before the show with the intention of doing some scientific tests. Behind a screen and wired up in some way to show a graph of her reactions, they had a woman with rheumatism in her knee. Then they had myself and a number of young men who looked like me come along in turn and touch the woman. This was done in a completely random way, with myself and the other men coming back again and again in a different order to touch her. The tests showed the graph of her reaction to my touch to be totally different from that of the others. It was also shown that when I was healing there were changes in my respiration and pulse rate, and in the electrical potential of my skin. During the show, one of the doctors who had carried out the test dismissed the findings and said much more research was required.

During the show, which was live, the host brought out a container full of worms saying that one of the proofs of the healing gift was that worms died when I touched them. They put the worms on my hand, and then ran a stopwatch to see how long it would take the worms to die. The worms died in seven minutes. A doctor on the show claimed that it was the heat of the studio that killed the worms – but after all, the worms had been in the studio long before and hadn't died. Was it pure coincidence they died after I touched them?

The money and the publicity and my own background led to other problems. I became the target for every con man in Ireland. Car salesmen and businessmen came to me looking for investment in their plans. I was a sitting duck – a country lad who had become a rich and famous national figure. If the people had any charm at all I was taken in by them. I think con men were drawn to me because they saw me as someone totally normal and thought I couldn't really be a healer. I reckon they thought I was swindling people, and that they in turn could con me. The few times I fell for them, I was severely burned.

I loved cars, and cars were my downfall. In Dublin I was introduced to a car-dealer. He was a real charmer, and he got my confidence, and said he was going to help me. I trusted him, but he turned out to be a ferocious con man. He made a huge amount of money from me, and he worked his way into trying to split me from my family so that I'd only take his advice. He could see how naïve I was, and he took full advantage of that naïveté. He was such a sharp man and was

dealing with such an immature youth, that he got money out
of me I never saw again. He'd make business deals for me
and he would sell me cars that afterwards turned out also to
be a con.

He once sold me an exclusive Jensen car from England. I
was driving it around, and one day Customs officers came to
my home and seized the car. It turned out that the vehicle
had been smuggled into the country with no import duties
paid. I was taken to court and charged with being in possession
of an uncustomed car – the story appeared in all the papers.
I couldn't get away from bad publicity.

This con man would introduce me to his friends, and none
of them ever warned me about him. Yet years later, I met
some of them and they said how bad he was and that they
would have told me but they didn't want to interfere.

At one stage, with stories about my money all over the
papers, I was nicknamed "Moneybags Nolan". One day
Brendan and I were driving from Sligo to Dublin after a clinic,
and there had been a bank robbery nearby. There were
Garda checkpoints everywhere, and all cars were being
searched. We were stopped at a checkpoint and the Garda
put his head in the window. He took one look and recognised
me. "Go on," he said, "you've too much money – you wouldn't
be bothered robbing a bank."

At that time, I felt that I could inform the media that I'd
resurrected the dead and they wouldn't be interested, but if
I were to say I'd had a new bill from the tax man it would
have been front-page news.

Money turned many people sour on me, and my fame was
tinged by scepticism. The idea that I was abusing my healing
power was expressed in a song Rory Gallagher wrote, called
Seventh Son of a Seventh Son, in which the man loses his gift
because he abuses it. I'll always remember how I first found

out about the song. I was in the toilet in Jury's Hotel in Dublin when a scruffy young man walked up to me.

"Aren't you Finbarr Nolan?" he said.

"Yeah."

"Our lead guitarist has written a song about you. He's Rory Gallagher."

Fortunately, my gift stood by me through the days when I was being so foolish, and, having travelled the length and breadth of Ireland with my work, I finally decided to take a step out into other countries to see if my gift would still heal people and if my success would grow. The further I moved away from Ireland in the following years, however, the harder were the lessons I learned before I finally came to terms with my life and my gift.

FOUR

Even though I had established myself as a healer in Ireland and could probably have gone on making a living as a healer here, my curiosity about the rest of the world finally got the better of me.

As I was holding clinics around Ireland, people were coming from England saying that I should go there. In particular, I was always being told that there was a huge Irish population in Birmingham and that many people there would come to be treated by me. Once, when I was down at the Rose of Tralee festival in Kerry, I met a man who was involved in public relations in Birmingham. He urged me to set up a clinic in the city and, in 1974, I finally decided to step outside Ireland and find out what the response to me would be.

I remember my first flight to Birmingham. As the plane came in over the city I looked down and I'd never seen so many houses before. I realised just how many people lived there compared to anywhere in Ireland and I was sure I'd get a huge response. I soon found out, however, that life isn't that simple. There were problems getting any publicity because the papers didn't accept what I did. When I arrived at my first clinic – fresh from Ireland where I was treating many hundreds each day – there were twenty people waiting to see me. In the course of the day I saw less than two hundred. Even the Irish newspapers mentioned the fact that so few came to me in Birmingham.

I contacted the local TV station, but when they researched a story on me they were interested only in the fact that I was in trouble for my taxes and in the end did an item which claimed I was in Birmingham trying to get away from my money problems. They did, however, include an item about a young man who had been cured of leukaemia – but this didn't add much to the numbers coming.

Up to that time, I had dealt almost solely with rural people. The experience in Birmingham showed me that being a healer or having the title seventh son of a seventh son meant nothing to urban people. The only tag that urban people had for me was "faith-healer", and since that hinted at the idea that being treated by me meant allowing themselves to be duped, the people of Birmingham kept away. I was sure, though, that having faith in me had nothing to do with my healing. I just had to let people know that my healing worked – independent of belief or any other trappings. As a young country man from Cavan, I probably seemed primitive in an urban setting. It was a barrier I had to break down if I wanted to reach people outside Ireland – but I just couldn't figure out a way of breaking that barrier.

I didn't want to give in, so I carried on working in Birmingham for a while. As I was holding regular, well-established clinics in Ireland I set up a routine for the Birmingham clinics which was exhausting. I would fly out there on Monday morning, hold a clinic during the day, and fly back that night. I'd do a clinic in Ireland on Tuesday and Wednesday, and then make another one-day trip to Birmingham on Thursday. Eventually I realised that I wasn't attracting the interest of the people in the area and so I had to move on. The surest way of reaching more people, I believed, was to go to the biggest centre of population and make an impression there. I had to convince English people that my healing gift was genuine and it didn't matter that I came from a tiny village and had been working in Ireland amidst rural people who believed in me as part of their folklore and tradition.

I went to London from Birmingham and I just concentrated on those who were most likely to come and spread the news by word of mouth – the Irish people. I placed an advertisement in the *Irish Post* there, but only about two hundred people showed up at the clinic. When I contacted the major newspapers they weren't interested, and I finally returned to Ireland to think about my approach. It boiled down again to the fact that if you have a gift you have to let people know you have it or they'll never acknowledge you. I decided that the only thing to do was to handle the whole thing professionally and hire a PR company. I didn't doubt my gift – I just needed to have experts get my message across to people.

The company I used was headed by a man named Fred Hift and they were very efficient. They organised the clinic and my publicity, and they generated a huge amount of media interest. As a result I attracted an enquiry from the BBC documentary series *Man Alive*, who wanted to examine the whole phenomenon of my work. I have never shied away from scrutiny, and I felt that this was the test to see how acceptable my work would be outside Ireland. I happily accepted their offer of making a documentary about me and the production was set up. I was convinced that if I could be a success in London I could be a success anywhere, and the documentary aimed at telling the story of how I fared.

I gave the *Man Alive* crew permission to film whatever they wanted and they followed me everywhere. They started with me at home and went to Dublin airport, boarding the plane with me to London. I arrived in London airport and the film crew were surrounding me and, as I moved into the terminal, there were about twenty journalists waiting for me and two TV crews. As I walked along the lights were flashing and journalists were asking me questions. The whole experience was dazzling and I remember a young woman working in the airport ran from her desk toward me.

"Who is it? Who is it?" she was asking as she tried to push through. Someone explained, and I heard her as she walked back to her desk looking very disappointed. "It's only some healer from Ireland," she told her work-mate. She must have thought I was a rock star.

There was a huge build-up to the first day of my clinic in London, and I was in the papers daily. As the clinic began there were at least a dozen journalists around me and many photographers. The *Man Alive* crew was there, as well as three other TV crews. To record me as I treated the people who had come, the TV crews had each equipped me with what's known as a radio microphone – a small microphone clipped to my shirt which led down to a small transmitter pack strapped around my waist, which in turn passed my voice on to the sound recordist. The result was that I had wires bundled up under my sweater. The reporters were talking to people after they'd been treated by me, and many patients said that my hands felt very hot. One reporter then noticed that I had wires dangling from my sweater and rushed to the *Man Alive* director to tell him I was a fraud and my hands were wired up to generate the heat. The director calmly explained the truth.

During the making of the *Man Alive* documentary, the cameras followed me for about six weeks. I told them they could film whenever they liked, and so they'd arrive at clinics and wait for people they might be interested in filming. On one occasion, a woman was sitting among the patients holding a little dog. The nearer I got to the woman the more intently the camera crew watched. Finally I came to her and she asked me to treat the dog. I explained to her that I didn't treat animals because legend was against my doing so. The cameras were close on us and I'd no idea what might happen. The woman accepted my point and left, but the reporter then interviewed me asking why I didn't treat animals and as I talked about what the legend ruled, I felt awkward about what I was saying. After that I decided there was no reason why I shouldn't treat animals. It was the last link I broke with the rules governing the myth of a seventh son of a seventh son.

I had a man managing me during the time of the filming, and it turned out that he wasn't as trustworthy as I'd hoped. I was paying him a set monthly fee for expenses, and I handed him a cheque for the amount due. He came back a few weeks later and said he couldn't find the cheque – he asked if I'd write out a new one and cancel the other. My brother Brendan fortunately stopped the first cheque, because a few days later both cheques came to the account. This incident and the strained relationship between this businessman and myself came to the attention of documentary makers, and in the end the film made much of how I was being managed and referred to the man as my "would-be manager".

At that time, Brendan was starting to become ill. We thought then that it was due to overwork and lack of exercise. He developed a slight limp, and the crew would watch him, always trying to get a shot of this. Brendan was very embarrassed by the matter, and when the documentary was finished there was mention of the irony that I could cure other people but not my own brother. That story was to develop unhappily in the future.

The highlight of the time in London concerned a young woman who was cured of blindness. A woman had come to me with her daughter, who was totally blind. I treated the daughter – she had damage to the optic nerves in her eyes. In the middle of a clinic a few weeks later the mother ran in, almost hysterical, saying I had cured her daughter's blindness. Naturally I was pleased to hear this, and naturally so too were the PR people who were working for me. Fleet Street reporters were contacted, but they thought it was a con for publicity. They interviewed and tested the cured woman, however, and when they realised her eyesight was perfect they tried to make out that she'd never been blind. Nothing could convince any of the newspapers to run the story.

The *Man Alive* documentary was still in the making, and the producers didn't know whether to believe the incident or not. I asked them to interview the young woman for the documentary and they agreed. When I contacted the woman, however, she said that she didn't like television and didn't want to appear in the film. I accepted her point and let the story pass – even though I knew that to have a blind person cured in the documentary would have been a major bonus to the film and to me.

Two months later, I got a phone call from ITN saying they'd been contacted by this blind girl who said she had been cured by me. Thousands of people were phoning up trying to find out how to contact me. I must admit I was disappointed by this turn of events. Although she hadn't appeared in my documentary the girl had sought her own publicity. Perhaps I've tended to be sensitive about publicity, but it's my lifeline and the only way people can find out about me. Two years later I met the cured woman with her mother. Her eyesight was perfect and she was looking extremely well. She'd just got engaged and was due to marry soon after. I was happy that her life was so much better and happier than it had been before she'd come to me. Looking back, I can almost understand how the British newspapers didn't report the story at first. The cure was so spectacular it was incredible.

In the midst of all the media coverage, I was seeing a thousand people a day in London. I was no longer the rural Irish healer, and I was treating people of many races and backgrounds. I was well known from all the coverage, and I was being stopped in the street by people who recognised me. In those days, I was at the height not just of my popularity but also of my fashion-consciousness. I had hair flowing down to my shoulders and I'd grown a beard. I dressed in the latest fashions, and at that stage I was driving my third Jaguar. It was then I got the tag of being the man with the Jesus manners and the Jaguar habits.

As I don't ask for names, I never know if I'm treating famous people that I don't recognise. One time, I had a clinic in a London hotel and the doorman swore to me afterwards that he had seen a prominent member of the royal family coming to me. Whether or not this really happened, I was once called to treat the daughter of a duchess and she was cured. Years later, indeed, the duchess contacted me about someone else she wanted me to treat but the nature and circumstance of the illness were such that I explained that I wouldn't be likely to be of any help and so the treatment was never arranged.

The mixed blessing of media hype continued through my stay in London. I appeared once on a BBC afternoon show, and they produced a can of worms for me to touch – this time, the worms didn't die. The *Man Alive* documentary mentioned at its close that the worms were still alive and well and living peacefully in Shepherd's Bush. I never thought much of the test, and when a journalist from the *Daily Mirror* asked me about the worms, I jokingly told him the power didn't work because the worms were English. He just looked at me very cynically and walked away. I don't bother with that test anymore. It led in the end to jeering, and I'm open to enough of that as it is.

As I was working away in London, at a clinic in Croydon, I got a phone call from CBS News in America. They asked me if they could do an item about me for *CBS Evening News*. That would lead to a huge amount of publicity, and I naturally leapt at the chance. The item CBS put together showed my background and the crowds at Gowna, and then moved on to show me at work in London. It was a follow-up to the original item, showing how my life had changed since my first success back in Gowna. They wanted to report on how a sophisticated place like London would react to me.

At one point during the filming of the item, they asked for a shot of me driving to the clinic. I was asked to drive about half a mile up the road and then drive down towards the camera. As I was driving down the road – with the camera filming – a car suddenly pulled out of a side road. An old lady got out of the car and came to me.

"I came to your clinic three times and I paid you three pounds and I wasn't cured!" she shouted. "You're an Irish con man. You're nothing but a bloody fake, and I'm going to report you to my local MP!"

The camera caught it all, and I imagined that the producers would use this to humiliate me. As it turned out, they didn't use the incident in the news item. I later found out that the woman was a member of a psychic society and the incident had been a deliberate ploy to embarrass me.

After the screening of the *Man Alive* documentary, I decided to open a clinic in the south of England. I was very restless in those days, and I wanted to see if I had gained a following away from the city and urban cynicism. I worked from a hotel in Brighton – the one bombed years later by the IRA during the Tory conference. Brighton, Eastbourne, and Bexhill-on-Sea were the areas I was covering. Bexhill-on-Sea is a town full of retired people. It was nicknamed the town of newly-weds and nearly-deads, and I was told that many wealthy people lived in retirement down there – although I saw little evidence of wealth. We used to have an expression for the money collected. If a lot of people had given small sums – coins – we'd say "there were a lot of rattles today". In Bexhill-on-Sea, we heard a lot of rattles.

One old lady came to me after I'd treated her and pressed a ten pence piece into my hand. "There you are," she said. "And if you cure me, I'll gladly give you another one."

The laugh we got out of the incident was about as much as was earned from the time there.

The travels in 1974 proved to be the last with my brother Brendan. He wasn't feeling well, and he was tired of always being on the move, and so from then on he settled down in Dublin while I carried on with my restless travels. When he stopped working with me I lost someone I could completely trust, but as it turned out there was something happening to Brendan that was more serious than we could have imagined. From that time on I dealt with different management people and had to cope with the whole process of learning who I could rely on.

Media coverage and success peaked for me in 1975. Up to then, anywhere I went – especially in Ireland – drawing five hundred people a day was low for me. There were times then when I'd go to towns and the Gardaí would have the

whole place sealed off, and for local businesses the passing
trade would suddenly go through the roof. There'd never
been anything else like it in Ireland. Newspapers were contacting me, and radio stations, and it was at such a peak that
I didn't even ask what paper the journalists were coming
from. I had wanderlust, and I had fame, and I had money.
Most of all, my gift was healing people.

Since that first process of establishing myself in England
I've gone back many times with varying success. In 1976 I
arranged to open a clinic in Liverpool. A month beforehand,
however, I was hurt in a minor car accident and my left hand
was in a plaster as I arrived to start the clinics. Reporters and
photographers met me at the airport, and they treated it as
an Irish joke to see a man coming to heal people while his
left arm was in a plaster. It was embarrassing, and the response
I got in the clinic was very bad.

During all this time my personal life changed very little.
For all my love of night-clubs and dances, I'd never had a
steady girlfriend. One night at a party in Dublin, just before
my twenty-first birthday, I'd met a beautiful young woman
named Caroline, who was an air stewardess. We began dating,
but between her job and my travels it reached the point
where we saw very little of each other and we finally broke
up after a few years.

So I was twenty-three years old, I had no ties and no respon-
sibilities, and I decided to travel the world. Healing people
gave me that chance. As the documentary said, I went back
to Ireland convinced that, as I had succeeded in London, I
could be a success anywhere in the world. London is a cynical
place, yet I was believed and people had come to me. In the
light of the documentary, the cures, and the continued
coverage, I believed the world was opening for me. On my
return to Ireland, and after the documentary was shown, I

71

received offers to go to Italy and Greece and Cyprus and America. If the world was ready for me, I was certainly ready for the world. My experiences as I pursued these new opportunities became more and more bizarre.

FIVE

I knew a man in Dublin who was a student from Cyprus. He had come across an item about me which had appeared in a Greek magazine, and he believed it would be a great idea for me to go to his country. His brother worked in promotions and offered to organise the trip, and since at that stage I was mad about travelling, I jumped at the chance. I flew to London and met my friend's brother. I spoke to him about going to Cyprus and he was very keen. The trip was set up, and he arranged work permits, advertising, publicity, clinics, and any other details.

Cyprus is a beautiful country, but when I went there, there were many refugee camps, and there was great poverty. There was also a strong army presence – Cyprus was recovering from a devastating war – and the United Nations were policing the peace between the Turks and the Greeks. I met a number of Irish soldiers there, in fact, who would read about me and come to have a drink with me. It was also easy for me to cope with being in such a foreign country because many Cypriots could speak English.

About three hundred people arrived at my clinic in Nicosia on the first day. I felt reasonably happy with the response, and looked forward to spending a pleasant time in Cyprus. Four days later, however, I was sitting in a restaurant being interviewed for a local paper when the police came in and arrested me.

"What's this for?" I asked.

"You're practising medicine without a licence," was the reply.

The journalist with me wrote down the details of the event as it happened. He had already met some people – one of them the head of the local taxi firm – who had been cured. For him, the incident was a scoop. For me, it was a shocking experience. To my amazement, I was put in handcuffs and marched out of the restaurant. As I was being taken to the police car, an old peasant woman came up to us almost in hysterics. She said she'd walked many miles to see me, and she implored the policemen to let me go. "Oh please, give us back our magic doctor," she cried.

I was taken down to the police station, and I didn't know what kind of trouble I might be facing. As it happened, I had newspaper clippings about me from all over the world in my briefcase, and when the police looked at these their attitude softened. They probably thought I was just some kind of a harmless freak. My promoter was contacted and he rushed down and posted bail for me. The matter was far from settled, though. I was told that I wasn't allowed to continue my work.

The incident blasted me on to the front page of all the papers and aroused national interest. The papers were very supportive of me, mainly because of the evidence of the head of the taxi firm who had been cured. The attitude was that I wasn't charging money, I was helping people and I deserved to have a licence to practise.

It quickly emerged that there was a huge demand for my healing, but I had to wait and do nothing while the government and the health minister considered my case. Pressure was building in the media to let me work, and everywhere I went, walking down the street, crowds gathered round me and sought me out.

"Come into my house! Treat my uncle! Treat my father!" they'd call out, but I had to tell them that I couldn't treat them until I was allowed do so by the government.

As the demand grew, one enterprising local ship-owner came to me. He suggested that we could fill his ship with people wanting to be treated by me and then take the ship outside territorial waters so that I could treat them. I didn't want to push the law, however, and decided it was best to wait for the official response.

While I was waiting for a decision about working in Cyprus, I was asked to go to a clinic in Nicosia which would be supervised by doctors. I was told that if they approved of my work I would be allowed to continue. A lot of people came and I treated them. The doctors obviously liked what I was doing because within a few days the licence was granted. After two weeks of being at the centre of media debate, the government made an announcement that they would allow me a licence to practise my healing in Cyprus for a month.

I was delighted to have gained permission, and I immediately arranged to open up a clinic the following Monday. At that stage I'd been news for the two weeks of the débâcle – but I hadn't realised just how big a stir I'd created. I had booked a room to work from in the Beverly Hills Hotel in Nicosia.

The room could hold about three hundred people, and was as much space as I reckoned I needed. It was a bright room – above a wall about four-feet high there was glass all the way round. At very best I hoped for crowds close to my early days in Gowna, but realistically I expected maybe a thousand a day would come following all the publicity.

As dawn broke on the first day of the clinic, a queue started forming outside the hotel. Soon there were thousands outside. As my day's work began, an incredible crowd of about fifteen thousand people were waiting outside the hotel to be treated by me. They must have come from all over the island all wanting to be treated before my permission to work expired. I felt frightened. Not only was I the focus of all this attention, and not only would it be impossible for me to treat so many people, but I also had no idea how such a flood of people would react to me. I remembered a story I'd heard once from a journalist about a healer in Italy who had been murdered by a man whom he'd failed to cure. Nothing could protect me from this desperate crowd if anything went sour.

I had a routine of seeing women first. Managing this was extremely difficult in the circumstances, and as we filled the room we'd have to bolt the door. Compared to the thousands waiting, the flow of people being treated was tiny. As the day progressed, the crowd became restless, and it came to a point where desperation set in. The people started smashing the glass to get in through the windows. Absolute mayhem broke out, and there was a real danger that people could be crushed to death. The owners of the hotel were in a panic, and were insisting I control the crowd and pay for the damage.

In the following days I worked to exhaustion but still couldn't see all the people who were coming to me. Where such a demand arises, there is bound to be an opening for tricksters and crooks. There were people going around with a photograph of me and a badge. They would take money from people in return for what they said was a booking to see me. The swindled people would form a queue outside my bedroom door in the hotel first thing in the morning saying they had appointments to see me privately.

Funnily enough, one of the policemen who had originally arrested me in Cyprus later became my friend and my only chance of security. He would take me out to dinner and sight-seeing, and act almost as a bodyguard. In return I would go to his home and treat a house full of family and friends.

Archbishop Makarios was the president at the time, and people would pretend they were his brothers and cousins in order to get into my clinics. I was afraid of falling foul of the authorities and so I'd treat them. Government ministers came to see me also, including the minister for defence. Even the attorney general came.

The whole thing was more than I could handle. I kept hoping things would become manageable but they didn't. In the end, I ran out of the country after a few weeks of this mayhem. It was either that or have a nervous breakdown. The impact I had was simply too great to cope with. It was madness, and indeed it was a poor country and so even though all these people were coming to me I earned very little. Between the promotion office and the manager and the expenses, in the end it was no more than a terrifying experience. As I was about to leave the country, the tax man came to me as well and I had to deal with him. I left Cyprus with little more than some very frightening memories.

In the end, though, I was delighted to get out. During the barrage, the hotel manager had told me that if there were an election, I could beat Archbishop Makarios at the poll. I think he was only half joking. Much as I want people to believe in my healing gift, I'd never wish for a situation of being held in such awe and being the centre of so much need.

After my return to Ireland my Cypriot policeman friend phoned me several times asking that I return. He wanted to start a new career working as my manager – I never even considered it. I'd had more than enough of Cyprus and I've never been back for fear of drawing the same response.

While working back in Ireland, I had a hard-nosed business-man handling my affairs. In 1976 he thought it would be a good idea if I set up clinics in Germany. I didn't agree with him at all – I believed that the Germans were very scientifically minded, and that they wouldn't go for my work at all. He encouraged me to try it anyway, and I finally agreed. He then organised a clinic for me in Hamburg through a German associate.

I arrived in Hamburg on Thursday and held a press confer-ence in my hotel. About four or five German newspapers sent reporters – I had hoped for television crews and radio interviewers and maybe fifty reporters. I sensed straight away that this episode was going to be a failure.

The following Monday I held my first clinic in Germany in a concert hall called the Winterhuder Fäirhaus. The clinic began at two o'clock, and as I made my way there I expected to find an empty hall. To my amazement, nine hundred people turned up. I just couldn't believe it. The people handling my business saw a big future in Germany because it was such a wealthy country and if this first day was anything to go by, the future there was very bright. What neither they nor I knew at that time, however, was that there were laws in Germany against what I was doing.

I worked in Hamburg for six weeks. Things were going extremely well – there were many cures, a good response to me, and goodwill from all the people. I liked the Germans so much and felt so at home that I even started learning the language.

The health authorities there, however, insisted on certain hygiene rules. They said that after every person I treated I had to wash my hands in a very harsh alcohol-based substance they provided. I only used it if I treated a skin complaint or a sweaty person, yet it was so severe on my hands that my skin peeled and became very sore. Two inspectors came again, and warned that I would be stopped from working if I didn't wash my hands after every person I touched. My hands became raw and I had to put soothing cream on them all the time to ease the pain.

We moved on next to Berlin. The German PR man went ahead and set up clinics and interviews. One paper said, "We know nothing about this man – has he ever cured anybody?" The PR man assured him there had been many cures.

"If you can give me one definite cure, I'll publish an item in my paper," was the reply.

So the PR man came up with Paul Tusher, who owned a motorbike superstore in Hamburg. Paul was a very serious diabetic, and after being treated by me he made such a dramatic recovery that he was taken off insulin. He was a businessman, he looked good, he spoke well, and he seemed to us to be the ideal case to present to the Berlin press. When we told the newspaper about him, they promised a front-page story. We phoned Paul to ask him if he would be interviewed. He said he was just back from holiday and was facing a backlog of work and wasn't sure if he could spare the time to go to Berlin. "Phone me back tomorrow and I'll let you know," he said.

Next day, we called and he had made up his mind. He agreed to be interviewed provided he was paid 2,000 marks and all expenses. For me, it was a bitter pill to swallow. I had cured him, and yet he saw his case purely as an opportunity to make some money. The newspaper kept their word, however, and the interview with Paul Tusher appeared on the front page. As a result, thousands of people came to me in Berlin. There were also TV and radio items about me. People were even coming across from East Berlin to see me – once people reached the age of 65 they were allowed to cross the border at certain times.

The crowds coming to me in Berlin were so big that a flower shop next door to the clinic complained. Their flowers were being battered around as people milled to get in to see me. The police came and spoke to my agent and there was no great problem. The police simply asked us to keep the crowds under better control – they even suggested that they would help us if we couldn't manage the queues ourselves.

Eventually I moved on from Berlin to Wiesbaden, which is outside Frankfurt. I couldn't get any publicity in Wiesbaden, but after two days there the police came to the clinic. They said that my work wasn't allowed in Germany unless I was a member of the Heil Praktische Gesellschaft – the association for healers and practitioners of alternative medicine in the country; mainly acupuncturists and homeopaths. They asked me to go down to the police station the next morning to give a statement, and told me that I had to stop working immediately.

My work in Germany had been going really well up to then, and suddenly that whole success was in jeopardy. I was so depressed and so disappointed, I went out that night and did something I don't often do: I got myself very, very drunk. I went to a bar with the PR man, and he introduced me to apple wine. I had no idea just how potent the drink was: I thought it was like cider, but it was more like dynamite. I drank maybe five or six glasses, and I don't remember anything after that. I was told afterwards that I had met a Yugoslavian in the bar who told me he had arthritis and I treated him. I met him a long time later and I had no recollection of him or the incident – yet he was cured.

I arrived at the police station the next morning in a very fragile state. The police took one look at me and smiled. "Ah – the apple wine," said one.

They photographed me and took my fingerprints and I made a statement. The situation was very clear: I could no longer work in Germany. I came back to Ireland feeling very disillusioned, thinking about the career I could have had in Germany. The interest in me had been great, and I liked living there, but without the licence I couldn't work.

I stayed away from Germany for a year, carrying on with work in Ireland and England. But in the end I couldn't resist going back. I didn't feel there was going to be any big problem, and there was such a huge demand for me in Germany that I foolishly believed it was worth taking the chance.

I'd been allowed to work in Hamburg on my first visit and the police there had been encouraging – even offering their help with queues and so on. So I decided to move far away from the trouble to southern Germany and open a clinic there. The response was good again, and I moved on through Germany. I worked in Hanover, Düsseldorf, and Cologne, where I treated the king of the Romanian gypsies. He came to me in all his finery, decked out in silver and gold. I moved on to Stuttgart and contacted the local papers. They interviewed five people who had been cured. Again, when the clinic opened, huge crowds came.

When I was in Stuttgart I hired a lawyer to find out exactly what my legal situation was. He contacted all the government institutions and they had no objections. He also contacted the head of the medical profession and they had no objections either. Only the Hiel Praktische Gesellshaft took exception to me, and were under the impression that I would be in competition with them. I didn't feel too threatened by their attitude to me.

I was working hard, seeing about six hundred people a day, and I felt things were back on track in Germany. In the middle of a clinic one day, however, I was called into a room and before me stood the police. I knew I was in trouble. They had a man with them, and he was saying, "Hiel Praktische, *ja, ja*."

At this stage I could speak a fair bit of German. I could tell from the conversation that he was trying to explain what I was doing and how I was breaking the law. I was arrested and taken to the police station, and the police were incredibly nasty. They told me I was practising healing without a licence and that it was an offence.

"What did I do? Is it serious?" I asked.

The policeman stretched out his arms. "Well, murder," he said, "that bad." He narrowed the gap. "What you do – this."

"Then what's going to happen?" I asked.

"Get yourself a lawyer," he replied.

I was handed a phone book under the listing for lawyers and told to pick one out. I did this, and the lawyer came to me in the police cell at about eight o'clock that evening. He spoke very fluent English with an American accent. I asked him my main concern – had I committed a serious offence?

"No, no, no," he said, "it's a minor offence. You'll probably get a year for it."

I nearly hit the roof. "A year?"

"Yeah, that's probably what you'll get."

I just broke down in tears. I lay in the cell that night trying to imagine what it would mean to spend a year of my life in jail for doing what I do. Freedom and travel had always meant so much to me and I had believed that my healing powers would offer me a life of seeing the world. Instead, I was facing imprisonment in a foreign country.

They woke me next morning and I was given the job of serving out the breakfast to all the other people being held in the police station. One policeman had lived in Canada for some time and he was at least pleasant with me. He gave me two books to read, which in fact were very gory thrillers and hardly what I needed to calm myself down. I spent a second night in the station, but was then released on bail. The police were making it very clear that I couldn't work there again, and I simply accepted the fact and returned to my hotel.

I was hardly back at the hotel when the police arrived and arrested me again. They brought me back to the station and I spent yet another night there. With my reasonable understanding of German I tried to find out what was happening with my case, but there were no explanations. On the third day, however, we were all taken from the police cells and put into a prison van. I remember there was a prisoner sitting opposite me with only one leg.

"Where are we going?" I asked him

"Stammheim," he answered.

I reeled at the thought. I figured I'd been sentenced in my absence and was about to begin my year in prison. The very thought of the prison I was going to stunned me. Stammheim Prison at that time was in all the newspapers. The leaders and other members of the left-wing terrorist group Baader-Meinhof were serving life imprisonment in Stammheim. The *Rote Armee Fraktion*, or Red Brigade, had kidnapped a major industrialist named Hans-Martin Schleyer and sought the release of twenty of their imprisoned members, but the government refused. The terrorists then hijacked a

Lufthansa plane and held the passengers hostage in an airport in Mogadishu, Somalia. German troops had gone out, stormed the plane and killed three of the hijackers, and freed the hostages. Three of the imprisoned terrorist leaders, including Andreas Baader, then committed suicide – though the Red Brigade believed they were killed, and in retaliation they murdered Schleyer.

It was into this situation in the immediate wake of these events that I was being brought to Stammheim Prison.

We arrived at the prison, a vast, grey place. We were all told to take a shower, and there was a warder going around measuring people for prison uniforms. Just then a prison officer came in shouting my name. "Nolan! Nolan!" I went to him and he stared at me. "*Du bish frei* – you are free."

I couldn't comprehend what was going on. I was left outside the prison, and they offered a police car to bring me back to the city. I refused and took a taxi back to the hotel. When I got there the people were very nice to me and very apologetic about what had happened. They wanted me to stay there for a while and rest to recover from the ordeal. But I just gathered up my luggage and got on board the next train to Switzerland.

I had gone to Germany to carry out my work as a healer and I'd wound up in the same prison as a terrorist group. I'd never felt so bitter. The police were so arrogant and the treatment I received was so unfair that I wouldn't dream of going back. The solicitor who had been representing me later told me that the police were angry that I hadn't been jailed. I can't even begin to imagine how I would have coped serving a prison sentence in Germany, and the memory of that prison still makes me shiver. Yet I met some lovely people in Germany and made many friends and I have long regretted the fact that I can't work there.

I learned later that what I do is banned in many countries in Europe – only professionally trained medical practitioners are allowed to treat people for illnesses. I obviously don't agree with such an attitude, and it's a limitation which prevented me from a great deal of travelling I'd hoped to do – I certainly wouldn't again take the chance of facing imprisonment by practising my healing in a country that doesn't accept what I can do.

SIX

I moved to Holland on my way back home from Germany. I had been on Dutch television in 1971, and on that basis it was a country I'd always meant to spend some time in. During my time there I got a great deal of publicity through a number of celebrities who had come to me. I had cured a Dutch actress, Teddy Schaank, and an actor named Johnny Kraaykamp, and a famous woman who had asthma. Interest in me didn't last for long, however, and I moved back home.

I was back in Dublin and carrying on with clinics around the country when I got a phone call one day from a woman in Milan in Italy, asking me to go there straight away – it was very, very urgent. I asked what the problem was, but the caller said that she couldn't talk as the matter was extremely delicate. Somehow, I had an idea that this was someone with cancer and that was why she didn't want to talk.

"Please come straight away," she begged. "I'll pay all your expenses and whatever your fee is."

I agreed to go.

I flew to Milan and a woman met me at the airport. She booked me into a comfortable hotel, saying she would call back later after I'd rested. That evening, she returned. I was expecting to be introduced to the ill person but instead the incident turned out to be the weirdest request I've ever had. The woman sat down with me and explained that her husband's mistress was pregnant – her request was that I end the pregnancy.

"I can't do anything like that," I said, "I heal people with illnesses."

She insisted that I'd be able to do it. "All you have to do is concentrate on the girl's stomach and taking the baby out of it," she explained. "A spiritual healer I went to before did the same thing with another girlfriend of my husband's."

Much as she coaxed, I totally refused. But this woman didn't take no for an answer. She told me how to go about imagining the baby taken from the womb. I couldn't believe what she was saying to me. Although I refused her point-blank, she asked me to stay in Milan for a while to think some more about it. In the following days she came and drove me around Milan and the region. She would only occasionally ask if I had changed my mind about her request – I always told her that I hadn't.

She seemed to be finally accepting my point of view, and she suggested that since I'd come all the way from Ireland it would be a shame not to visit Switzerland, which wasn't too far away. I agreed, and we set off out of town until we reached the main highway. She then started driving faster and faster until we were travelling at over a hundred miles an hour. I sat beside her in the front seat with my hands clutching the dashboard so tight my nails must have sunk into it. I was sure we were both going to die, and I realised she just didn't care.

"Are you concentrating on the girl's stomach?" she asked.

"Yeah, yeah, yeah," I lied desperately, humouring her and hoping that she would calm down. Believing that I had ended the pregnancy, she slowed down. After that experience, all I wanted to do was go home. She brought me to the airport next day and I went back to Ireland in a state of disbelief. The man who was managing me at the time thought he'd heard everything until I told him about this incident.

Back home, life became more and more difficult and my past was slowly but surely catching up on me. I have always presented myself as a healer, but I was never a businessman and I'd accumulated problems through my lack of financial sense. In the mid-1970s, amidst all the travelling and healing, I was under mounting financial pressure and was taken to court over the tax bills to appeal against all the assessments made by the tax office. I had never organised anything as formal as a fee in my clinics, and my income was chaotic. Apart from Germany, my work outside Ireland hadn't earned much money. But in Ireland I was believed to be a rich man. In court they asked me how much I was earning and I said it was very little. Then they said they'd sent five people to my clinics and all five had donated a pound per visit. I said that didn't represent an average, but they insisted it did.

The cases dragged on and my court appearances weren't handled well. They would demand figures, and would ask, "How much did you earn on such a date?"

"I don't know," I'd reply, "I didn't count it."

"Well, who did count it?"

"My brother counted it." And the court would be adjourned for my brother Brendan to appear next time.

I didn't know how to deal with it, and the clouds gathered while all I could think of was that another week had passed without a final bill being presented to me. What I didn't know at that stage was that if the tax office believe you owe them money, they will definitely get it. It had reached a point where I was being assessed for a total income of £700,000. It might seem from the outside that I was living a high life, but I was staying at home with my parents in an ordinary Dublin house when I wasn't travelling abroad with my work.

The whole matter was getting very serious, and my accountant in Dundalk decided that the matter required legal action. He put me in contact with a firm of solicitors. They noticed straight away that I was being assessed while a case was sub judice for another assessment. They wanted to take this to the Supreme Court, believing they'd win. Their plan in fact was to bring the matter to the brink of going to the Supreme Court, and then settle at the last moment with the tax office for a lower figure. But I knew it would mean that my name would be blasted all over the papers and the idea of that kind of publicity scared me and I backed off. The solicitors were furious.

As the pressure increased, I decided the whole thing was going too far, and sought a way of settling out of court. I was recommended to go to an accountant from Leitrim, and he turned out to be a disaster. He went in and agreed a deal with the revenue commissioners which left me having to pay them every penny I'd made. He even made deals for £25,000 for years in which I hadn't earned any money.

In the midst of the court hearings leading up to this deal, the revenue solicitor came up to me and asked me how I'd come to choose the accountant I was using. I explained that he had been highly recommended to me.

"Well, I'll give you one piece of advice," he said. "Get rid of him. He's an idiot."

The final sum I paid was £54,000. In the mid-1970s, that was a huge amount. I had difficulty paying the revenue commissioners the money because I really didn't have it. Even so, I paid them and felt at least that was the end of the matter. Since an agreement had been reached, I got rid of the solicitors in Dundalk, who then sent me a bill for £9,000. I couldn't believe it and refused to pay because I didn't accept that they merited such a fee for what they'd done. They also hadn't received written permission from me to take the court proceedings they'd begun.

My brother was advised that the best approach would be to take their bill to a legal accountant. He was told that once the legal accountant made a final decision, that amounted to a court order and the sum decided had to be paid. As it turned out, the legal accountant said the sum due was £4,000. I dug my heels in and still didn't agree with the sum and so I wouldn't pay. What I didn't know then was that there was no way out of paying once the legal accountant's decision had been made. The solicitors threatened bankruptcy on me but I reckoned they were bluffing.

During all this, I didn't notice the stress the money worries were bringing on my parents and family. The case was all over the papers and I think it embarrassed them. At the time, my father was in his late seventies and my mother in her early sixties. Probably the only sensible thing I'd done with my money was to buy a home for them. One Sunday afternoon, a man knocked at their door. He said he knew the house was going to be sold because of the bankruptcy and he wanted to know how much of an offer he'd need to make to buy it. They slammed the door on his face, but they were very upset.

Despite all the troubles – or maybe because of them – I kept on wandering around the world whenever an opportunity arose. I was working in London and some foreign correspondents wrote about me, including one for a magazine in Greece. One day, I got a phone call from British Airways saying they had two tickets for Athens in my name. I said I knew nothing about it. The next day came a phone call from people in Athens saying they had arranged the tickets. They wanted me to go there and treat a woman who had multiple sclerosis. I went over, all expenses paid, and when I arrived three or four hundred people showed up to be treated by me. I decided to return later and spend some time there. It seemed like a good way of escaping the mounting financial problems at home.

For legal reasons, the only way I could work in Greece was through a doctor's surgery. A Greek film actress I had treated introduced me to two doctors who agreed to take me into their clinic. The doctors were practising acupuncture, and the agreement was that after people had been treated by me, the doctors would ask them if they wanted acupuncture treatment. As it turned out, the majority of people declined the offer.

One day, a woman was carried in to me. Because of the language barrier, I didn't know exactly what was wrong with her – it seemed to be rheumatoid arthritis. The next day, the same woman walked into the clinic saying she was cured. I went to one of the doctors to tell him about this, and he refused to believe me.

"It's not possible," he insisted, throwing his hands up in the air. "I go to school and I work very hard to qualify to cure people – how can you just put your hands on people and cure them?"

While I'm abroad, I always like to buy an English newspaper – mostly for football. I picked up the *News of the World* in Athens one Sunday and there was the news about me: "Faith Healer Bankrupt", was the headline. I hadn't known anything

91

about it until then. In the end, it was the solicitors who made me bankrupt in 1977. The tax man came in on top of this with an extra assessment of forty thousand pounds. It was a disaster for me, and I didn't know what to do.

No one knew where I was at the time, and there were messages going out to Irish embassies all around the world trying to contact me. I made up my mind not to get in touch with home, and decided to stay in Greece – working there, yet not knowing what to do with my life.

Working with the two doctors didn't prove an easy relationship. When a TV station came to do an item on me, the doctors insisted that a large emphasis be put on their acupuncture work. The TV programme refused, and the item never happened. The doctors had taken me in as a way of increasing their own business, but when that didn't happen they asked me to leave.

When I left Greece, I went back to Holland where I organised my own PR for the first time, contacting papers and magazines. I was operating alone and taking care of my own affairs – there was no one else I trusted. Every major newspaper and magazine did articles on me and I hoped to attract a lot of people. It was very difficult to have them take me seriously, though. The seventh son of a seventh son meant nothing there, and I had a poor response despite cures which were reported in the newspapers.

I spent six months in Holland, during which time the petitions against me for bankruptcy were being processed and I was being sought to face up to the debts. I found out that attempts were being made to arrest me in Holland but couldn't be carried out. During my time there I met an American named Jack Harte. We got along very well together, and we remained in contact after that. I talked to him about my interest in going to America, and he believed that I would be successful there. Jack was to play an important role in my life later.

In the end, I knew I couldn't stay in Holland. I missed my home and my family, and I realised that I'd remain an exile if I didn't face up to the hard facts. I finally decided to return to Ireland and go to court. It was time to face the consequences of my years of naïveté and come to terms with my debts. I arrived back in Dublin and began the process of becoming a bankrupt. I set up clinics, but it was a demoralising period in my life because people were no longer breaking down the doors to get to see me. Crowds were dwindling and I thought I was finished as a healer. All I could imagine was a time when I'd be penniless and have no way of making a living. I wondered what kind of job I could find for myself, since I had no other qualifications – I hadn't even finished secondary school.

I told the official assignee that I was doing well in Holland and he agreed to allow me my passport so that I could go back and work. I worked in Holland for a further month and brought back only six hundred pounds. It was another terrible blow, and when the reality of my situation sunk in I became more and more depressed. For three months I hung around, doing nothing and feeling very low. I couldn't bear to face the fact that I'd been so irresponsible with my gift, and I just sat back and let the days roll by.

Finally, one day I was lying in bed and a strength suddenly came back to me. I'd had enough of being out of control and I decided to get my life in order.

"Right, " I said to myself, "I'm going to go out and I'm going to sort myself out and get rid of all the debts and put all my troubles behind me." It was probably the first time in my life that I took my career and my gift seriously. If I could heal

people then they should know about it and I should be able
to make a reasonable living from doing what I could do.

I went out and started doing clinics again throughout
Northern Ireland. The crowds were good, and for the first
time I recommended a charge on my work of two pounds
per visit. People didn't seem to mind the fee and there were
no complaints. To my mind, if I was a fraud people wouldn't
have come to me at that time and that would have been the
end of me. Despite all the publicity that had gone before about
money and tax, there were enough people who had heard of
the cures to come to me believing I was a genuine healer.

I was on the road again, determined not to look back.
Things would get better, and I decided to build on my successes
instead of dwelling on my failures. I'd grown up a lot through
the whole experience and learned a lot of hard lessons. In a
strange way the bankruptcy took the pressure off me. When
you become bankrupt, you don't exist as a person. The official
assignee became Finbarr Nolan. If people owed me money or
I owed people money, the official assignee dealt with the
matter. I became very angry about the bankruptcy: I felt I
didn't owe the money I was being bankrupted for, and I was
very bitter. It was a time in my life that I just wanted to put
behind me and forget about – I had to forget about it for my
own sanity. Thinking about it even now is hard: it was a
terrible period in my life. It was a bad dream, but I got out of
it. I went on and made a comeback – a lot of people couldn't
believe the comeback I made.

I had a very good relationship with my bank manager and
when I finally went to see him, he couldn't understand why I
hadn't gone to him earlier.

"We would have lent you the money," he said, and in the
end it was the bank who wrote a letter saying that if I was
released from the bankruptcy they would guarantee the

payment of the money due. They knew I was honest and wasn't going to con them, and they knew the whole problem had been caused by immaturity on my part.

At that time, too, I finally decided to clean up my appearance. I shaved off my beard and trimmed my long hair. When one of my friends, Matt, saw me he said, "You know, when you had that long hair and beard I used to wonder about you."

It hadn't really occurred to me before that I was going around looking like a modern-day Jesus – I thought I was copying the Beatles.

At the same time, things were going well for me in Northern Ireland and I was very heartened by the way people trusted me. I was doing a clinic in Larne once when a doctor burst into the room and told everyone that they were wasting their money and that I was a fraud. Some of the men who had come to see me rose to him, and the hotel manager had to come and take the doctor away to avoid a fight breaking out.

There were still the disappointments too, but I had to accept them. In 1978 I treated a girl for epilepsy in County Down. The night that I treated her she had a very violent attack and her mother contacted me. I assured the mother that it was a very good reaction, and indeed it turned out to be the last fit she ever had. When I later asked her if I could use the story for the newspapers, she declined and suggested that in fact she'd been cured at Lourdes.

Despite the cures and the new order in my life, there was a growing cloud on the horizon for the family. Brendan's illness had become very serious. He had reached the stage where he had difficulty walking, and any remedies he tried for himself – more exercise and so on – failed to change the situation. I finally persuaded him to go to a doctor, even though he didn't believe in them and thought the problem would pass. He was tested and diagnosed as having multiple sclerosis.

It was a shock for all the family. I couldn't believe it had happened.

Brendan was convinced that I could cure him. Every time I went to see him he'd say, "Come on into the room now and do the job for me. You can do it. I know you can."

I was always reluctant about treating him. For some reason, I feel very uncomfortable about treating members of my family – it's as if some block comes up. But Brendan really wanted me to treat him, and I'd treat one part of his body, and the next time he'd ask me to treat somewhere else. There was no sign of an improvement, but Brendan was sure that it was just a matter of finding the right spot to treat. I ended up treating him over and over again, but nothing happened. He eventually ended up in a wheelchair. I could do nothing but watch it all happening.

As for the bankruptcy, I set all that aside as I started to look to the future. I believe the whole affair resulted from sheer stupidity, immaturity and ignorance on my part. Now that I'm older and wiser, I always pay my taxes and my accounts are kept in proper order at all times. That lesson is one I learned the hard way, and the idea of going bankrupt again is probably my greatest fear.

A long time afterwards, a man came up to me and said he worked in the tax office. He said, "I'll just tell you one thing. If you'd never had a Jaguar, or mentioned money in the papers, the tax people wouldn't have come after you the way they did. People were constantly phoning up asking us to investigate you and saying it wasn't fair that you were getting away with not paying taxes when you had so much money."

Indeed, a few years later while I was working abroad, I came back to Ireland on holiday and a man came to the door asking me to treat him. I asked him how he knew I was home.

"I have a sister in the tax office," he replied, "and someone

Finbarr's paternal grandfather
who was known as 'the Doctor'

Finbarr aged two,
around the time of his first cure

The tiny, sleepy village of Gowna where Finbarr grew up

Snapshot of the huge crowds which surrounded the Nolan home in Gowna

At work in a clinic at Arvagh in the early days

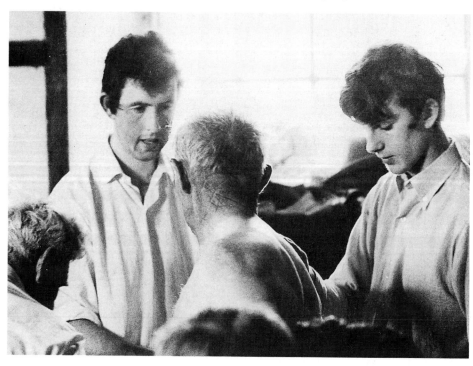

Finbarr aged 17, known throughout the country as 'the boy with the healing hands'

*The cures continued in the travelling clinics around Ireland as word
spread about the young healer*

*Demand for his cures was so great at Balgriffin in North County Dublin
that a special bus service had to be organised to transport the thousands
who wanted to see Finbarr*

Finbarr comes out of one of the many court hearings on tax which plagued him in the early 1970s

Now that he is a father himself, Finbarr is even more aware of how precious children are

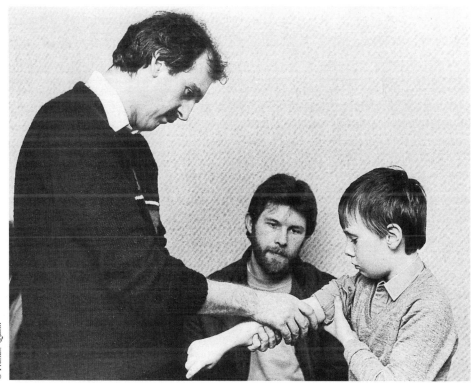

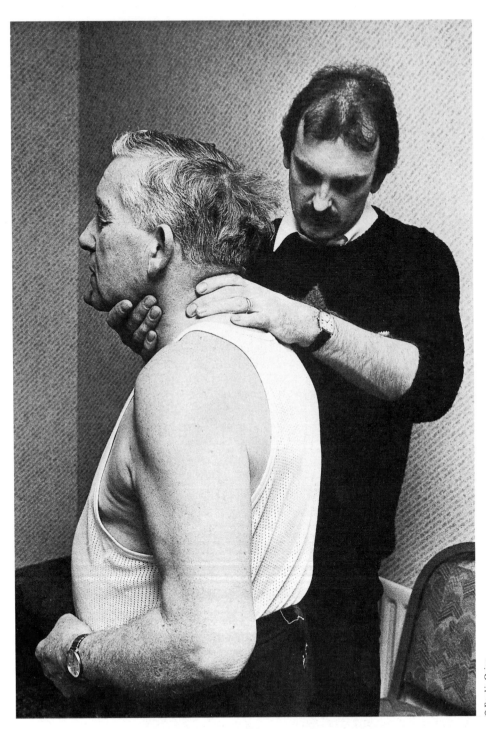

Finbarr treats people of all ages for whatever condition they may be suffering from

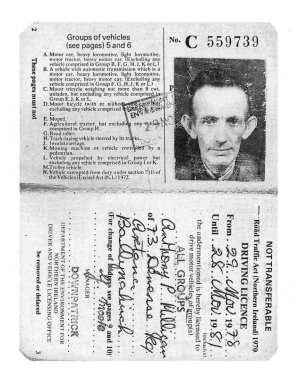

The story of Anthony Milligan is probably Finbarr's most spectacular cure

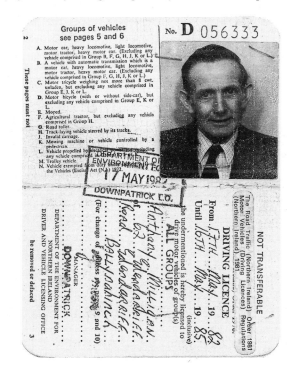

called up there to say that you were home and to make sure you were paying your taxes."

As I was earning money and re-establishing myself in Ireland I was also planning my greatest adventure. As my name was cleared from the bankruptcy, I was free to leave the country. I knew where I was going – I was heading for America and for a leap into world recognition for my healing powers. I saw the time coming for a move to new horizons. I had been through the times of being a rural Irish healer. I had been through the times of being labelled a faith healer. As I accepted my fate, I decided that I should set the gift its ultimate test: America beckoned and there, I believed, I would face the challenge of achieving international recognition.

SEVEN

I had been wanting to go to America for years, particularly since the second CBS item about me when I was in London. Everyone said it was the place to go, where I'd be believed instead of being treated with scepticism. "You'll make millions!" I was told, and I saw a future with managers and agents and sponsors. I believed that it would transform my life and bring a vast number of people seeking my healing.

I wanted to go to New York, and I had two options for getting there. I had remained in contact with Jack Harte, and he was going to help me establish myself there. But I'd also met a man in Dublin who said he could make all the arrangements to set me up in America. In the end, it was the advice of this man that I took. There were delays about getting a work permit and a visa, and it seemed like years were passing without the move happening. Finally in September 1979 I just got on a plane and went to New York.

The night I arrived I booked into a hotel on Broadway. I met a man at the bar there who was friendly and chatty, and we went out for a meal later on. I walked along the streets of New York chatting to him but mostly preoccupied by the incredible height of the buildings. I suddenly received this thwack across the chest. A stoned black man stood before me. He'd hit me with his umbrella. "What are you looking at, you son of a bitch!" he yelled at me.

This was my welcome to New York. I had thought that London was the toughest city in the world. I soon had my eyes opened: New York was a thousand times tougher.

I went to a management company on Broadway who accepted what I did and drew up a contract to represent me. A clinic was organised in the Queens district of New York in an Irish ballroom. The feeling was that the Irish population in New York alone would create vast crowds coming to me, and advertisements were placed in the *Irish Echo*. The agents were discussing having bodyguards for me, such was the expected demand.

I had also hired a PR firm, and the woman dealing with me had said she could get me into the newspapers and on loads of shows. Her fee was $1,500 a month. She phoned me later, saying, "We have fantastic news here. This show interested, and this TV show, and this radio show, and this newspaper."

I was delighted. "Who do I talk to? When does it happen?" I asked.

"Well, pay me my fee first and then we'll discuss it."

So I paid the fee straight away, but no shows were mentioned after that.

I was nervous and excited about my first clinic in America. I had been convinced by myself and others that the Americans would flock to me. The talk had been of bodyguards and crowd control. I arrived at the ballroom which had been hired to find it was a dusty, musty old place – and less than ten people showed up. I was deeply disappointed.

For all the dealing with PR and agents, on the night of the clinic only two journalists came to the event. One was from the *New York Daily News*. As I sat in the empty ballroom being interviewed by this reporter I tried not to seem too upset. He was asking me about my age, my background, Ireland and so on. Then he said, "Were you ever in jail for all of this?"

I nearly jumped about ten feet off the seat. "What do you mean, in jail?" I said.

"Well, for conning people."

I got really angry and things between us became very heated. I only discovered afterwards that he'd been sent through the work of the PR company – and he was a crime correspondent for the newspaper.

Working as a healer in America turned out to be a complicated matter. I found out that, because of the danger of lawsuits, I always had to have a witness present while I was treating someone. The witness would be male when I was treating a man and female when I was treating a woman.

For historical reasons, there were also legal limitations on where I could work. In the nineteenth century a healer had set himself up in California and thousands flocked to him. It was discovered that he was a fraud, and as a result a law was passed saying that you could only heal people if you were a doctor or if you were acting in the name of God, forming your own religion. So my kind of treatment is against the law in many states in America, and the bible-thumping healers have grown largely out of that law.

My clinics in New York continued, even though their attendance was very low. I moved to a clinic in Manhattan and worked away hoping that word would spread. The next thing I heard was that I was being interviewed on *The Tom Snyder Show* – a nationwide programme which came on after *The Johnny Carson Show.* I hoped this would be a big break and that I'd get some attention in America. On the night, others on the line-up included Paul Simon and members of the Hell's Angels. I appeared on the show with two people I'd cured – a woman with arthritis and a man with psoriasis. Even though everything went very well, Tom Snyder never said a word about where I was working or how people could contact me. I found out afterwards that their switchboards were jammed with enquiries but no information was passed on.

It was a huge opportunity lost. Even worse was the fact that around this time I was contacted by a doctor who was based in New Jersey. He recommended that I move down there, suggesting that people would find my base in New York very inaccessible and that would put them off. I took his advice, and moved to a place called West Long Branch, but I soon found it was a mistake. I'm sure I would have been better off staying in the centre of New York.

The first patient I had in New Jersey was a man whose wife had a stroke. At that time people paid voluntary donations, and sometimes people wouldn't give anything until the third visit. This man was leaving with his wife after the third visit and said to me, "Thank you, Mr Nolan. If you cure my wife, I'll pay you."

Things like that had never happened to me before and I was shocked by the mentality. For the most part, though, I found that the people were well disposed to me. They liked the fact that I asked for donations rather than setting a fee.

I moved on after New Jersey to Philadelphia. In Philadelphia, a woman came to me with cancer of the uterus. Two weeks later she went back to the cancer specialist and he said, "It's unbelievable – the whole problem has disappeared."

A friend of this woman came to the clinic and, as usual, I asked how she'd heard about me. She told me about the cure, and I thought that this, at last, might be what I needed to get some credibility in America. I asked for the woman's name and address, but the friend declined until getting permission. The following week she returned and I asked if she would give me the information.

"No," The woman replied. "She doesn't want to give it. She says she came to you and made a donation each visit and was cured. Since she's stuck to her side of the bargain, you should do the same."

I was constantly trying to figure out ways of making some kind of impression on the Americans. One silly little approach that backfired was the time I told staff in the hotel where I was staying that my name, Finbarr, was a very rare and special Irish name and that I was called after the patron saint of Cork. A few days later, a young black man came to the hotel looking for a job. The receptionist called me over and said to me, "Here's someone you should meet, Mr Nolan. His name is Finbarr."

I'd been in America for three months and things certainly weren't going well. At the end of another day of a mediocre clinic, I went out to my car and found it had been broken into. Everything was gone – luggage, money, papers. There seemed to be no end to the setbacks.

I moved on then to Baltimore, and was about to go back to New York when I met Jack Harte again. By that time I had no one managing me. I had stayed with the original company until I discovered that my manager was into cocaine. I remember one time in the office he fainted and started pouring with sweat after taking some drugs. Some time later he had a heart attack and died. Jack and I had got on well since our first meeting in Holland, and when I met him again he convinced me to go with him to Miami where he owned a restaurant. He thought Miami would be a good place for a clinic as a lot of old people lived there.

Jack reckoned that the way to launch me in Florida was to do something that would make a big impression. He arranged for the mayor of Mirmar to invite me to the town and to have a civic reception to greet me. The mayor, a man named Joe Veins, agreed and on the first day of my clinic there was a press conference held and all the TV news crews were there. I thought this showed great interest in me, but I was virtually ignored. They'd come to attack the mayor.

"Why did you invite someone like this to come here?" they were asking. "It's not very upright to invite a healer to our town."

Veins roared at the reporters and told them about my success around the world. He said he wanted his citizens to have the benefit of my healing, and that it was a disgrace that people didn't believe in me. At the next municipal elections, however, Joe lost his position as mayor.

Jack organised a contract for me with the William Morris Agency – the world's biggest. Unfortunately, it never went further than that. They did nothing for me and all I had to show was my signed contract.

In the midst of all this I had an unexpected break away from America. Jack had a friend in Monte Carlo whose wife had cancer. I was asked over to treat her and so I travelled there and was booked into the very luxurious Hermitage Hotel. I treated the woman every day, and spent the rest of my time wandering around Monte Carlo without taking much interest in the casinos.

I got a phone call from Jack saying that *The Merv Griffin Show* – a very big show in the States – were interested in talking to me. He gave me the number of a researcher to contact in California and I did so. Unfortunately, I forgot about the huge time difference and phoned him at what would have been the crack of dawn there. He was extremely gruff.

"What can you do?" he barked down the phone.

"Well, I cured a girl of blindness."

"Big deal – what's so great about that?" he snapped back.

Nothing ever happened with the show.

In Miami a lot of old people live in condominiums. Jack thought it would be a good idea to contact the various presidents of the condominium associations, give a presentation explaining my healing powers, and hopefully reach the residents that way. So we paid for a cocktail party in Jack's restaurant, with free food and drinks for all. As is normal, the refreshments were served first. There was no shortage of people for the food and drinks, but as soon as we started doing our presentation the people would leave – they were out the door like a bullet. As these efforts to establish me continued, Jack introduced me to a man who became not only my road manager but also an inspiration – Vinnie Marcesi. Vinnie had been a millionaire and a show business manager in the 1950s, and his acts had seven records in the US charts. He also married six times, and each divorce cleaned him out financially. When Jack introduced me to him, he was broke.

Vinnie was the most persistent man I'd ever met. He was full of life and enthusiasm and he was unstoppable. He was often given the job of getting a story into a newspaper. He had the capacity to just hound newspapers into submission. If he went one day and they said no, he'd go back the next day offering them another way of looking at the story. If that failed he'd go back the next day and the next. He simply didn't take no for an answer. He'd virtually exhaust the editors.

One particular time, I had three PR men trying to get a story about me into the *Miami Herald*. They had failed, and we decided to let Vinnie try. Jack told him to go down and be sure to see the editor, even if it meant bringing a camp bed with him and waiting outside the office until he finally made contact. The final result was a page and a half article in the *Miami Herald*.

I learned a great deal from Vinnie. He used to say, "Well, people are not going to buy it if it's locked away in a closet. You have to show them and tell them about it."

He used to look after me, organising interviews and doing all my publicity. He'd be at the clinics, liaising and talking to people, answering any questions they might have. He was a totally no-nonsense kind of guy, a real New Yorker. Sometimes, though, he wasn't the best person to have dealing with people coming to me. One day a man came to the clinic and asked Vinnie if he could see me privately. Vinnie, in his usual gruff way, said he couldn't: "What's the matter anyway?" he barked.

The man explained that he was impotent and he didn't want to be treated with others present.

Vinnie wasn't the sympathetic type. "I'm sorry, sir," he said. "Mr Nolan only deals with the living. He can't raise the dead."

Jack, too, was a joker. Vinnie would give his talk to people who had come to the clinic, and it was a set piece. Just as he'd near the end of his speech – a job he hated doing – Jack would arrive with people he was keeping outside, saying, "Hold on, hold on – there's two more people here," and Vinnie would start all over again from the top.

Jack believed in me and thought I would establish a great career in America. He told me at one stage, however, that people thought he was mad getting involved with a healer.

I discovered that in America being the seventh son of a seventh son meant nothing. In interviews they'd ask, "How come you can heal?" and I'd explain that I was the seventh son of a seventh son. They would just raise their eyebrows. Lots of people were being cured – the problem was convincing Americans that I had healing powers.

Jack was interested in exploring my healing powers and tried various little experiments. He kept track of my results over a certain period, checking to see if the phases of the moon had any influence on what happened – but there was no difference. He also had a friend who owned a pyramid-shaped house and Jack arranged for me to treat six people there whom I hadn't previously been able to cure, in order to see if the combination of my healing and the legendary powers of the pyramid shape would affect the results. But there was no change.

Jack introduced me to a fellow Irishman who was incredibly sceptical about my healing. His name was John Reilly. John had an extraordinary laugh, and when he was told what I did he dismissed the whole notion as a joke. John, however, had suffered for years with a bad back and he had to wear a steel brace. He was coaxed into coming to my clinic and I treated him, even though he was sure nothing would come of it.

One night some time later, I saw John in Jack's restaurant. I went over to him and I put my hand on his back just to feel for the brace – he wasn't wearing it. I asked him how he was feeling and he said his back was still giving him hell. A week later I saw him again in the restaurant and again realised he wasn't wearing the brace. I told Jack about this, and he confronted John.

"Finbarr thinks your back is better and you won't admit it," Jack said.

John burst out laughing and admitted that since seeing me he had been free from pain. John had a friend named Lorraine who'd had migraine headaches for forty years. He told her she should come to me, and when I treated her she was cured too. John later became a friend of mine and managed to lose his cynicism. He would even recommend that people come to me.

"Go to Finbarr," he'd say. "What the hell have you got to lose?" Of all the gloom that came out of America, at least I made friends like John.

Jack convinced a millionaire friend with a back problem to let me treat him. His attitude was typical of Americans as far as my healing gift was concerned. I showed up at his mansion to see him and I was cleared by the security men and taken in by the butler to treat him. Coming back for the second visit, I asked him if he felt any improvement.

"You know," he said, "it's about eighty per cent better – can you just imagine how I'd feel if I believed in this bullshit?"

I faced animosity and scepticism all the time. I had no problem getting on to talk shows on the radio because people found what I did was so controversial. Time and again I'd sit there and streams of calls would come in from people abusing me and mocking me. It was very disturbing.

I was invited up to Washington to take part in a radio show called *The Larry King Show*. It went out to a network of about four hundred radio stations throughout the USA. The night before I was on, the former US president, Gerald Ford, had been interviewed – that was the level at which the show normally operated. Larry was a friend of Jack's, and he spent the first twenty minutes of the show justifying my presence by saying how credible and brave a man Jack was. I was on the show for three hours, taking calls from people all over the US.

One wise guy phoned up and said, "Larry, I can't believe you have this guy on."

"Mr Nolan, why don't you go to Africa and heal them over

there?" another caller asked. "We don't particularly want you in this country."

Larry picked up on this. "Supposing he doesn't want to go to Africa?" he said.

"I think he should go there," the caller replied. "They need him there more than we do. We don't want him at all. I mean, he can't talk properly or anything and I don't know why you have him on the show. I wish I could get a job like the one he has."

"Well, maybe you could," Larry said, "Perhaps you might try Nairobi."

It was always the same. The Americans didn't want to know about me. My American dream was fast turning into a nightmare.

EIGHT

My chance to finally reach the Americans and gain some credibility came through treating not a person, but a racehorse named Poverty Boy.

I had treated a man who had a retina problem and he was cured. He had heard me on radio saying I'd had some success with animals, and three months later he came back to me, asking if I would treat a racehorse he part-owned. It seemed the horse had great potential, but it had a bad back and a shortage of breath.

I went out and treated the racehorse, touching him as I would normally do, and the following Saturday he came in joint winner in a race. It seemed to me that this could be a big publicity move – just what I needed to make some impression – so I asked the owners for their permission to publicise the story. They were very reluctant, back-tracking because they didn't want to draw attention to the horse and thereby affect the odds, but nevertheless a TV news item mentioned the win and that he had been treated by me.

Then we contacted a major TV show called *Good Morning America* and told them about the story. Their answer was exciting and gave us great hope – they agreed to give a ten-minute spot to the story if Poverty Boy won his next race. The show had an audience of close to a hundred million people. Finally, there seemed to be a chance of reaching America.

Jack, John Reilly, Vinnie and I went to Florida's Gulf Stream race-course to see the race, even though the owners were saying that the horse appeared no better. We all had a bet on the horse, and had a great day – this was one of the largest horse-racing events in America, the Preakness Stakes. The race started. Poverty Boy took off and he was about fifty yards in front. As the race progressed, however, he fell behind. He wound up finishing in his usual position – last. He simply hadn't the stamina to outrun the other horses because he'd been sick for so long. The odd thing about the whole affair was that the owners denied my involvement and claimed they were using a drug treatment. Yet I met the part-owner ten years later and he told me Poverty Boy had gone on to win several races after that fateful day.

"You cured that horse," he said to me.

To top it all off, the wife of the vet who was treating the horses in the stable heard about my involvement in the affair, and she claimed that the horse had been faith-healed.

The psychology of the Americans remained a mystery to me. I was in Jack's restaurant one night and we were chatting to a woman we'd met. Jack was explaining to her about my work and my cures.

"Imagine," he said. "This guy cured a girl in London who was totally blind, and he got a dollar for it. Now Julie, if you were blind and somebody restored your sight, how much would you give them?"

"Oh," she said very definitely. "You mean to say if I was blind and somebody restored my sight? Why – I'd give them fifty dollars."

Jack and I retreated to his office and we broke out in convulsions of laughter.

Another opportunity to gain wider recognition came when I was invited to appear on a TV show in Florida called *Montage*. The host was a lawyer named Joe April. The show was pre-recorded, and Joe wanted to interview anyone who had been cured. We brought along three people – one of whom was a woman who had been blind through diabetes, but whose sight had now returned. Another was a man who'd had cancer, and who had been given the all-clear. There was also a woman who had been crippled with arthritis but who could now walk normally.

Joe April interviewed me, asking the usual questions about how it all started and how the healing worked. Then he talked to the three cured patients. At the end of the interviews he asked them, "Were any of you paid to say what you've just said?" and they all replied that they hadn't. Everything went extremely well, and I felt that something very positive would be going out on television. But for some reason the show was never screened.

We tried to find out why but all we got was dead silence; though they had the proof in front of them, they obviously just didn't believe it.

Jack and I used to joke that maybe the reason the show wasn't transmitted was that the man who'd been cured of cancer was named Frank Mafia.

We had opened a clinic near the airport in Miami, where a lot of Cubans lived and there was a Cuban radio station. I was interviewed on the station by a man named Thomas Ricolados. I had treated him for migraine – a condition from which he'd suffered for thirty years – and he was cured. As a result, hundreds of Cubans turned up at my clinic. One day six hundred people turned up. This seemed like some kind of progress, but at the end of the day Jack said, "This is ridiculous. You've seen six hundred people, there are all these expenses and all this work, and you're hardly earning anything. You're going to have to set some price."

It was something I'd never thought of before and I was very reluctant to agree. In America I'd been operating the same approach to payment I'd always done. People paid whatever they wanted and only if they wanted. That, however, just wasn't working – Americans prefer to only pay what they have to pay. In the end I came to terms with the fact that the American trip had never gone well, and I decided that this at least might lead to some kind of financial reward for the work. I'd reached the point where I had to decide either to charge or just pack up and go home: I simply wasn't earning enough money to cover my costs. When I finally decided to set a fee, I suggested a donation people were expected to give. I was very scared that people would reject me for setting a fee, but I simply had to cover my expenses and make a living. I decided on a price of ten dollars. Jack thought I was joking. He said that any other healer in the field of alternative medicine would charge two hundred dollars. But the price I set was as much as I wanted to impose.

This ten-dollar charge resulted in terrible resentment; there was almost a riot outside the door of the clinic when people were asked to pay. But we stuck to our guns, even though the numbers dwindled considerably. I was later invited back on to the Cuban radio show, and as we were on air abusive calls poured in from people roaring and screaming at me in Spanish, complaining bitterly about the fee I was charging. Some even started to storm into the studio. People were furious about being charged a fee and then not being cured. In the end I had to leave the area. The Cubans felt that they shouldn't have to pay for any service. For me, it was coming to the point where my work in America had to either earn me some money or come to an end.

From my base in Florida I had occasionally travelled out for stretches of work in Georgia, Palm Beach and Tampa. The next step, it was felt, was to move on to the city of Altanta in Georgia. There was a very big population, and as CNN (Channel News Network) was based there, there seemed to be scope for good media coverage.

The timing of my arrival, however, was totally wrong. Black children had been disappearing and no one could solve the case. There were even psychics from all over the world trying to help the police find the culprit. Atlanta is about ninety per cent black and the amount of animosity between the blacks and whites reminded me of Northern Ireland. The crimes, of course, made things worse. It seemed as if the black community was just waiting for the word to be announced that a white man was committing the crimes.

Into this I came, and the animosity towards me was incredible – it bordered on hatred. I went on a radio chat show hosted by a blind black DJ. He struck me as being a religious freak, and he didn't believe in me at all. "I'm blind. Cure me if you're so good," he said to me.

"Right. We'll try it," I replied.

"No," he said. "I don't want to be cured – I'm happy enough the way I am."

When people phoned condemning me, he'd encourage them and agree. But if anyone phoned to make a constructive point, he'd just press the button and cut them off. In the middle of the show, Vinnie could contain himself no longer. He stormed into the studio and took me away.

"You don't have to take that nonsense from that son of a bitch!" he snapped.

This was happening live on radio. We stormed out of the place, and as a result of the whole incident I got maybe five hours of coverage on the radio, with others talking about the incident. In the end, however, very few turned up at the clinic.

While we were in Georgia we contacted the TV stations, and CBS responded with a proposal.

"We have an angle here," they said. "We have a famous basketball player, Tree Rolands. He has a bad knee and he's been out of action now for the past year and a half. If you're interested, we'll arrange for Finbarr to go and treat him."

We agreed to the idea and went to the Atlanta Hawks Stadium where I met Tree Rolands. I'm over six foot tall, and it was the first time in my life I felt like a midget: he towered over me. We went into the dressing-room and I treated his knee, which was very badly swollen. I came back for the second of the three visits the following week.

"Well Tree," I said, "how's the knee?"

"It feels completely better," he replied. "The swelling has gone down and the pain has stopped."

I thought that at last the break had come for me. We contacted CBS with the good news and they were delighted. "We'll meet you there at eleven o'clock tomorrow morning," they said.

The next morning, however, there was no CBS. It seems they'd contacted the team doctor and he dismissed my treatment. Tree Rolands, though, showed his gratitude. He gave me a basketball with "Thanks for all your help, Tree Rolands" written on it.

After that incident I left Atlanta; I could see I wasn't wanted there. I went back to Florida, but my time there was very mediocre. It certainly wasn't what I'd anticipated at the heady start of my adventure in America. I'd thought they'd be beating down the doors to reach me, but I could never get through the wall of scepticism.

Despite all this, it was in America that I was finally studied in detail by two experts in their fields. Summaries of the studies can be found at the end of this book.

The first study arose through my being interviewed by the *Miami Herald*. As often happens, after the interview the reporter then sought out a scientist's response to my work. Instead of going to a medical doctor, however, the interviewer consulted Jack Kapchen of the parapsychology laboratory in the University of Miami. He was very positive about what I did, having previously studied healers in South America. He had also studied spiritual healers in the USA – the bible-belt gospel-thumpers whom he'd exposed as frauds. He would attend healing sessions held by these preachers and watch the frenzy as someone who hadn't walked in twenty years would be touched by the preacher and then rise to their feet. Jack would try to follow up the story – looking for names and addresses and medical histories – but he was always turned away.

As a result he was sceptical about me and asked for a meeting. I was the antithesis of the kind of healers he'd met in the States – I gave him lists of names and addresses of people I'd cured. He was taken aback by this, and he agreed to do experiments on me at the university. I went to him once a week for five weeks so that he could carry out his tests. He had me immerse my hands in water and then fed plants with that water to see what the growth rate was like. He also took Kirlian photographs of me – photographs which show the electric field around all living things. He tested my psychic ability with cards. Unfortunately, the tests weren't fully completed because of time restrictions.

Another man, Robert Willner also did a study, which I believe is probably the most significant piece of work on my healing. He had me treat people who didn't know who I was or even that I was healing them, and his results said a lot about my capabilities. Dr Willner published his findings and was interviewed about me on radio. His colleagues in the medical profession thought he was crazy, but if anyone criticised him he'd repeat, "I'm only stating exactly what happened in the experiments." He stood by me no matter what kind of scepticism was expressed.

Despite these studies, the media coverage and the cures, the main response to me in America was resentment. I had opened a clinic in Tampa, and I was doing a radio show there the day I started. As usual, unfortunately, I was receiving a constant barrage of cynical phone calls. I tend to think now that Americans treat radio chat shows as a chance to be abusive and to just let off steam. It was as if the country were full of furious people just waiting to get their anger off their chest.

In the middle of this show in Tampa, a woman phoned up and said, "You're going to get yourself into trouble, boy."

"What?" I said.

But she just replied, "Wait till you see. You're going to get yourself into trouble."

That day the police came to the clinic and arrested me. The offence I'd committed, they said, was that I worked as a business without an occupational licence. The licence itself was a formality and a very minor thing.

One of the policemen was very polite and apologetic. "We have to put you in handcuffs," he said. "We know you're not a hardened criminal, but the state law says you have to be handcuffed when taken into police custody."

So I was taken from the clinic in handcuffs and into the police car. I was held in the station until I bailed myself out with two hundred dollars and went back to the clinic. Of course, I wasn't allowed to practise, and next morning I went to see a lawyer about the whole affair.

He was outraged by what had happened and convinced me that I could sue the state for my arrest. He said I'd get compensation for the embarrassment and the defamation of character, and rhymed off the charges he would bring against the state prosecutor. Foolishly, I lapped up the whole thing and got caught up in his frenzy.

"By the way," he said, "to start the ball rolling with these applications and so on, I'm going to need a thousand dollars."

I handed over a cheque.

"Come back in the afternoon," he said, "and we'll discuss this further."

When I came back in the afternoon he'd changed his tune.

"They're dropping the charges," he announced. "It was a mistake, and I reckon you'd best just go home and forget about it."

I didn't see the thousand dollars again. My stay in America was a constant succession of such failures and blunders. A politician friend of Jack's reckoned afterwards that being arrested for not having a licence was an over-reaction and that the police were probably responding to a crank phone call.

This was not the end of the bizarre incidents. Once, in the Miami clinic, a South American man was brought to me in a wheelchair. He had been shot, and nobody needed to tell me why – he was plainly a drug dealer. When he arrived it was as if the President of America himself had arrived: he had about fifteen bodyguards around him and bullet-proof limousines were lined up outside. I treated his wound and then forgot about the incident. A week later, I happened to glance at a TV while the news was on and my attention was drawn by the sight of a wheelchair lying on the ground near a limousine. There had been a murder in south Miami. It turned out that the man I had treated was at the centre of a gang war. The assassins had failed in their previous attempt to get him, and he'd come to me probably hoping for a fast cure. But he'd been tracked down and shot the following week.

I had moved to America in 1979. By 1981 I knew it was time to leave. My intention, when I left the States, was to take a break in Ireland and then return to work my way down into South America. Even more so than the Irish, there is huge belief among South Americans in the whole idea of healers.

The last time I was on a radio show in America, a man phoned asking why I didn't go into hospitals and heal people there.

"Suppose I went into the hospital and you were lying there in your bed," I said, "and I went over to you and asked you if I could treat you – what would you say?"

He just hung up. It was that scepticism that made me weary of America. On the one hand, despite so many television stations and newspapers available, it was almost impossible to make an impression on people. On the other hand, if you did make an impression they reckoned you were trying to get something from them so they shut you out.

I went back to Ireland in February 1982 and my plan was to work there for about six months and then go back to America. I was going to go on from there to Mexico and a Mexican promoter had been hired to organise the clinics. If the American dream hadn't turned out as expected, we thought that perhaps South America would yield more success.

As I was working in Ireland, however, I met Caroline again. We had been dating for four years when I was in my early twenties, but then she had gone her way and I had gone mine. I bumped into her one night and we decided to have

a chat for old time's sake. This was three weeks before I was
due to go to Mexico, and I never imagined that it was going
to affect my life. When we met, however, we discovered that
the old attraction hadn't diminished. My feelings for Caroline
were still the same, just as hers were for me. Neither of us
had ever met anyone else that we were so attracted to.

I'd often felt that my line of work would turn women off
me, but Caroline didn't feel that way. She helped me feel that
my work wasn't the most important thing – she loved me for
myself. We saw each other again, but then we parted when I
set off for America.

I went to Miami, all ready to take on South America. I was
staying with Jack during the short time it took to finalise
arrangements for Mexico. I was talking to him all the time
about Caroline, and I'd phone her and chat for ages. She
was a hostess on flights to New York, and sometimes I would
fly up to meet her for the day. Soon Jack realised that my life
was changing and that I'd met someone who was really
important to me. He finally sat me down and said that maybe
it would be better if I went back to Ireland for a while until
the arrangements for Mexico were better organised. Looking
back, I realise he was diplomatically acknowledging the fact
that I'd fallen in love and maybe my travelling days were over.

When I came back to Ireland, Caroline and I decided to
marry. It meant the end of the American dream (which I
think of nowadays as the American disaster) but it was definitely
the best thing I ever did in my life. It's possible that if I hadn't
met Caroline I would be living in South America today – but
my life now is much better and makes me far happier.

Before going to America, I'd listened to all the people
who had said that I would be a huge success there. I'd fallen
for the notion that the Americans are open to new ideas and
believe in what I do. I found them to be the opposite. I found

them cynical and very hard to get through to. Everybody there has something to sell, so everyone's defences go up. The biggest problem was that my being the seventh son of a seventh son meant nothing to them. They were sarcastic and cynical about the whole idea. The husband of the woman I cured of diabetic blindness, for instance, had mentioned the cure to his workmates. I found out later from him that he stopped talking about it in work because he was jeered so much.

"I was getting so ridiculed and abused I just stopped telling people," he said.

Jack Harte managed me in America and he was a totally honest and good man. He really liked me personally and was interested in me, and perhaps the greatest thing he did was to stand by me even when things were bad. I've had plenty of experiences of people conning me and taking from me; Jack was the complete reverse. He brought me into his home, he helped me when I had no money, and he never lost faith in me. By the end of my stay in America my finances were very bad, yet Jack helped me out. I think of Jack as my American father, and I have remained close to him ever since that time. My greatest gain from my time in America was finding such a friend. If it had not been for him, I'd have left America a lot sooner because of all the nastiness and disappointment.

As for Vinnie, he's now selling life insurance in Florida. The job is notoriously hard, but I can't imagine a better man than Vinnie to take it on.

I was married in September 1984. We invited about sixty people to the wedding – including, as a gesture of friendship, Jack Harte and John Reilly, although I didn't expect them to come because of the distance. After the wedding ceremony, as I walked down the aisle with Caroline, I saw Jack and John sitting together in the last pew smiling at me. They had flown all the way from Miami. I nearly died of shock, and I was delighted that they paid me the compliment of coming to my wedding.

Alternative medical treatments have become much more acceptable in America now. I was there at a time when the attitude was that the only cure you could have was from a pill or a doctor: no other cure existed. They didn't believe in anything aside from the mainstream. It was only a year or so later that alternative medicine started making any impression on the American mind. That was too late for me. I had worked out my wanderlust and chosen Ireland as my home. I certainly have no regrets about that choice.

Maybe all these things are for the best. I matured a lot during my twenties through the travels and the bankruptcy and the attempt at success in America. I suppose I wouldn't be the same man today if I hadn't tested myself, and the mixture of success and failure taught me a lot of lessons.

NINE

When I settled down in Ireland in the 1980s, things went very well and there was a high attendance at my clinics. I had a new approach to work, and I was determined not to repeat any of the old mistakes. My tax was in order, I managed myself, and I was in control of my own work and practice. I was a lot more mature, I'd learned my lessons and, as a married man, I wasn't going to create any of the old problems. Nowadays, as far as management goes, I'm a bit better than I used to be. Certainly, I have a totally reliable accountant and solicitor. I keep records of what I earn and I keep records of my cures. I pay my taxes and it's in my own interest to handle my affairs as a family man rather than as a young lad wanting to live the high life.

The days of the thousands of people thronging to me were over, but I got back to work as a travelling healer and I was content to carry on with the work I was born to do. The cures continued, and I was building a home life for myself.

Caroline was often teased by her friends about marrying me. They would say that she'd never be ill, and she would tell them that she was the healthiest woman in Ireland. My personal life is very happy. Marrying Caroline was the best thing that ever happened to me. We have two sons now – Barry and Shane. Becoming a father made me much more aware of the sadness of illness in children and I'm now even more moved by treating children than I used to be. People sometimes ask me if I'm going to have seven sons and, quite apart from how Caroline would feel about the matter, I can assure you that I'll never do that.

My mother is a great support to me at all times. I imagine that during the bankruptcy episode she had many difficult times with dirty looks and people talking behind her back about the trouble I caused, but she always stood by me. She's a very strong woman, and for her the family always came first. She's a very loyal and true person. If not for her, I'd never have been a healer. If she had said no at the start and refused to accept the legend, my life wouldn't have been the same. She kept up my strength through many hard times.

I began a regular circuit of the country, and in 1983 my travels brought me back to Cavan, the home of my discovery. The last time I'd been there was 1972. This was the county in which I had experienced the peak of my success. It was also the very root of my reputation – before all the media attention, people from around Cavan came to me in a regular quiet flow for years. The local press reported my arrival with great excitement and it was expected to be almost like a reunion. Ironically, the clinic was a disaster. Very few people showed up, and I felt I had parted company with my home county. Perhaps they had come to associate me too closely with all the bad publicity of my early days.

Although the 1980s were years of new-found happiness in my personal life, there was also much sadness. Brendan's condition became very much worse and it started to affect his breathing, eyesight and speech. All the while, he was convinced that I would heal him. I kept on trying, urged on by his faith in me. His illness was to become another one of the hard lessons in my life about my gift and my fate as a healer.

My brother died of multiple sclerosis in 1984. His death was painless in the end, but it was very sad and it upset me very much. In the heady early days Brendan had been my right-hand man, and it was he who had been with me through everything from the planks and barrels outside the house in Gowna to the media frenzy in London.

On the day of his funeral, a very strange thing happened. I had a prearranged clinic in Whiteabbey, just outside Belfast, and I had to go there after the funeral. As I was working a woman came up to me. I'm happy to say that it isn't unusual for me to have people come to clinics telling me that I have cured them. On this particular occasion the woman was delighted to inform me that since being treated by me in London in 1974, her multiple sclerosis had been halted and she was enjoying good health. The doctors couldn't understand it, she said.

It taught me a painful lesson to have my brother buried the same day with the very same disease. I felt that God was reminding me that the gift came from Him and not me. Certainly, if I could have had my way the rôles would have been reversed and my brother would have been the one in good health. But I have no say in how the gift works. Sceptics have described what I do as faith-healing, but when I look back on Brendan I know that if ever anyone had faith in me it was him. If I could have had any control over the gift I would have healed him.

124

In 1985 I had a very big scare about my own health. I was in Manchester doing a clinic and I woke up one morning blind in my right eye. At first I thought nothing of it, believing it was a virus that would go quickly. I went to bed early that night and I slept, thinking the problem was being caused by fatigue. Next morning, however, my sight had not returned in my right eye.

When I arrived back in Dublin I went to the hospital to have it checked out. They arranged for tests the next day and carried out a brain scan, a CAT scan and blood tests. They then sent me to a specialist in another hospital where tests were made on my legs and arms. They told me they were looking for the symptoms of multiple sclerosis since the problem with my eye was a sign of that disease. They wanted me to come back to have a lumber puncture performed, and I just got out the door of the hospital and never went back. My sight returned, and I never suffered any recurrence of such effects. The experience frightened me very much, though, and gave me some idea of what it was like for my brother to be told such news.

More sadness came in December 1989 when my father died, just a few weeks short of his ninetieth birthday. He was a good, solid man and he had lived a full life. At least there was some consolation in knowing that he wasn't taken before his time.

My life has become a constant flow of time spent away from my home and family in hotel rooms. I've grown accustomed to the routine, and I just get in there and do it, treating my work positively. My gift is my job and my life. I have the same ups and downs about work as anyone else, but that's life and I accept it.

I work to a five-year cycle and when I go to an area I hope to reach everybody there who might want to come to me. Leaving a five-year gap means that anyone who wants to see me at that time has been treated, and by the next time there would be either a new set of people with ailments or people I've seen before coming back with other problems. It gives plenty of time, too, for recommendations to spread by word-of-mouth. Many of the people who come to me now do so on the recommendation of people I have treated before.

My routine is to book a place somewhere for the clinic – usually a hotel room – and then place advertisements in the local press giving details. Usually it is older people who come to me.

I do a lot of work in Northern Ireland and get a very good response there, whether in a Catholic or a Protestant town. I never ask anyone to give their name, nor do I ask their religion, and I find that's the best approach to take. I have always been accepted in the North, but the Troubles there have meant that I have to be conscious of the sensitivity some people have about my work in loyalist areas.

Recently in a clinic in Antrim I was asked to go downstairs to see people in wheelchairs. Before me were two people – as it turned out, one from Shankill Road and the other from Falls Road. It struck me that in illness they were united. They shared, also, the wish to be healed.

One of the best cures I ever had was a young girl from the Shankill Road. She had cancer of the spine. The doctor had said that he could operate on the condition, but if he were to do so she'd never walk again. So her parents took her to me, and within a few days the growth disappeared. It seemed that it would make a great story – a news editor's dream – and I asked the parents to publicise the case. But the parents didn't want the name used, as they were worried by this cure of a Protestant girl by a Catholic healer. The parents were very grateful, however, and I understood their sensitivity about the matter.

A similar thing happened when, in Bangor in 1985, I cured a boy of deafness. The story was an ideal one for the newspapers: the boy had been born deaf, and his hearing had been restored. Unfortunately, his parents wouldn't agree to any publicity.

In 1987 I had a clinic in Belfast and three members of a family asked me to treat their father who was suffering from pancreas failure. I explained that I couldn't go until the following Tuesday, and they said he would be dead by then. I dropped everything and went out to the hospital with them. The man was in intensive care, unconscious. I treated him, but as I left the unit I turned to his family and just shook my head. I couldn't see how I'd be of any help.

I had arranged to meet them the following Tuesday in the hotel, and when I arrived there was no sign of them. I immediately thought that the man had died. That evening, while I was holding my clinic, one of the sons came in.

"I didn't really expect a result," I said. "He was very seriously ill."

To my surprise, the man told me that his father had come out of intensive care and was recovering. I was delighted with the news.

"We think you had a part to play in it," the man added, and I asked him who he thought had actually cured him.

"It was his belief in prayer, and all the people who were praying for him that cured him", he replied. I felt it was a snub of my work and I was annoyed, but in the end it has to be accepted that what really mattered was the man's recovery.

Once, in Omagh, the *News of the World* came to my clinic and while they were there a man who had a paralysed arm was suddenly cured. The reporter and photographer seized upon the story. About two years later, another journalist and photographer from the same paper arrived at my clinic and were disgruntled because there was no spectacular cure that day.

Even though the majority of my work is done in Ireland, I still go to England and Scotland and occasionally America.

In Liverpool in 1987 I was asked to see a man with lung cancer. He had been given two months to live, and had been told that there was no medical solution for his condition. I treated him in his home, and that night he was kept awake with severe chest pains and a desperate burning feeling all over his body. He told me afterwards that he'd cursed me for whatever I'd done to him. In the following weeks, however, he made an incredible recovery. He regained his appetite, went back to work, and his life seemed to be getting back to normal.

In my opinion, however, the doctors made a serious mistake by taking him back into hospital for chemotherapy treatment which they thought he had become strong enough to cope with. His health started to fail once more, and when I was called to see him again I remember that his room was full of bottles of tablets. I felt the drugs would do him no good, and sadly he died not long afterwards.

My work has remained contentious, and the benefit of the doubt is something I'm rarely granted. I was barred from seeing a boy in a rehabilitation centre in Dublin. His parents had asked me to go to him and I'd agreed, but the doctors wouldn't allow me in. That kind of attitude continues to hurt me, but my work is my work and I just carry on.

At least in more recent years I've seen changes in the attitude of doctors towards me. Recently a man came to me suffering from Menier's Disease, which affects the hearing and balance. He told me that he was being treated by a specialist who said there was nothing he could do for him but that he knew of a previous patient who had been cured by me.

Over the years I've been involved in some unusual treatments. The most unusual was the time, about twenty years ago, when I was asked to go to a hospital in Meath where a man was dying with hiccups. The man was in intensive care because the strain on his heart from the hiccups was killing him. The hospital authorities wouldn't allow me permission to treat him, and I had to be smuggled in. He was totally drained when I got there, and after my third visit he'd recovered completely.

I've also crossed paths with some well-known personalities. There's a pub in Aungiers Street in Dublin called The Swan Bar. It's a family pub run by Sean Lynch, who played rugby for Ireland in the early 1970s. As a result, particularly on the night of an international, a lot of rugby people go to this pub. One year Ireland were playing France and Tom Grace was the captain of the Irish team. Tom was carried off the pitch due to a knee injury with only half an hour to go. I was in The Swan Bar with some friends when a number of the team, including Tom Grace on crutches, came in. When I was recognised, they coaxed me into treating Tom. We went upstairs and I treated him, and to my surprise he immediately felt better. He threw away the crutches and was able to walk normally. But he was so embarrassed by the cure that he slunk out of the pub rather than show his team-mates. As it happens, his knee was sore again the next morning and he didn't come back to me.

In 1983 I got a phone call from the athlete Eamon Coughlan, saying that he had trouble with the Achilles tendon in his foot and he wanted to be fit for the World Championships in Helsinki. I treated him, and he subsequently won the Helsinki 1500 metres – three months after I treated him. I read later that he said his Achilles tendon had been cured by a German doctor. I often wondered if I'd had anything to do with the cure, but even if I did I never got any credit for it.

I've always attracted incredible scepticism. People can't understand that someone with the power to heal can also go to a bar, or go to a football match, or dress and behave like anyone else. People expect me to be in some way out of the ordinary, but I'm no different from anybody else.

I was giving a clinic once in Killarney, and as usual I asked if anyone had been to me before. One woman said I'd cured her brother of Hodgkin's Disease and that he was now back at work. Later, I asked the group if anyone had any questions. The lady sitting with the woman whose brother had been cured put up her hand.

"Excuse me," she said, "I was just wondering if you've ever cured anybody?"

I realised then that no matter how I tried, there's no way I'm ever going to be able to convince everybody of what I do. Obviously, even seeing is not believing.

I was at a party once and in the course of the night three or four people approached me and asked if I'd ever cured anyone. I was so irritated that when I got home I went through my files and approached the *Sunday World* with twenty testimonies from people cured by me. The editor published the article, and I felt it was at least an attempt at letting people know that I'm not a con man, not a faith-healer, and that, yes, I have cured many, many people.

My most disappointing case involved a priest who had leukaemia. I treated him in hospital, and he started to make what seemed like a very good recovery. I had a friend in the newspaper business, and I told him about this priest. The journalist published the story, and it stated I'd said that without my cure people would be reading about the priest in the obituary column. I don't remember saying that. Later, the priest died. I felt very disappointed in myself and very ashamed about the fact that the story had gone into the newspaper. His family never contacted me again, but I imagine they were offended by the article. I regret that situation very much.

It taught me, above all, to be very careful about cures of cancer. On a number of occasions I have treated people with cancer and they have made marvellous recoveries only to suffer a relapse. I was reminded again through the incident that I can't say someone is cured until they are consistently better for a substantial length of time.

A few years ago I was asked to go over to Canada to treat a woman who was dying of brain cancer. I was reluctant to agree and I also wasn't free to drop everything and go. Her relatives pleaded with me, and I finally went. When I was met at the airport and taken to the hospital the little hope I had of being able to help faded away. The woman was lying there like a vegetable: she couldn't talk or move, but was motionless and helpless. I thought to myself that this woman needed a miracle, and that her relatives had been completely unrealistic in bringing me over.

I treated her then, however, as well as on the following two days, and left Canada feeling that I couldn't possibly have been of any help to the poor woman. Six weeks later, I got a phone call telling me that the woman had regained consciousness and was out of hospital. She wasn't completely cured, but she had made great progress. She was able to stand and walk around on crutches. I was elated by the recovery she had made.

They asked me to come back and treat her again. This isn't unusual, because I've seen a lot of cases where people get a noticeable amount of relief from one set of visits and then gain even more from a further series of treatments. This is especially true if someone has responded to what I did initially. With this woman, however, there was no extra relief from any further visit. She later came to Ireland for further treatment, but again, unfortunately, there was no improvement. The doctors told her husband, however, that her recovery had been extraordinary and that they hadn't expected her to leave the hospital alive. She died some years later, but at least she had been given some extra time and life.

I usually leave Ireland once a year, mostly during the winter months since I don't like to travel the Irish roads from week to week in miserable weather. I usually go to London or some other English city and I draw a reasonable number of people. I was in Scotland in 1974 and had a very poor response then, but in November 1990 I decided to try again to see if the response would be any better. I expected to spend no more than six weeks there. Instead, reports of cures gathered a great deal of media attention and the crowds have grown and continued to the point where I spent over a year commuting from my Dublin home to Scotland every week.

Ireland remains my stronghold, though – especially rural areas, where belief in the legend together with word-of-mouth recommendation about my past work keeps people coming to me. I will usually be visited by more people in a small Irish town than I would be in a city of a million people. I hold private clinics in the Irish capital but Dubliners have always been sceptical about what I do. My gift has its roots in country superstition and seems to have little appeal amongst city-born people. Those who come to me in Dublin are very often rural immigrants to the city.

As times have changed, I have also come into contact with more unusual challenges and have found new possibilities for my healing. In 1988 I got a very desperate call at home one Sunday from a Dublin woman who wanted me to treat her daughter. It was a very unusual story. The girl had been in the USA, and her father had taken her to a hamburger joint. Shortly afterwards she became violently ill. This lasted several days, so her parents decided to cut short the holiday and bring her home. The girl's condition deteriorated, and no treatment worked. She was taken into Crumlin Children's Hospital, but still there was no response to treatment. In the end, the doctors could hold out no hope.

The girl's parents asked if I would come to see their daughter, but I was just back from working abroad and was about to head off again the following morning, and I simply couldn't spend more time away from my family. I told them the earliest I could see the girl was the next Friday.

"It'll be too late," they said. "She'll be dead."

Unfortunately, there are times when I must draw the line, otherwise I'd have no private life. I felt, in a sense, that if I'd been contacted earlier rather than once panic had set in, it would have been better all round. The following Saturday, they brought the child to me. The girl was skin and bones, and her body was covered in a severe rash. Her eyes were glazed, and I could see she was dying. I treated her, and asked her parents to bring her back the following Saturday. When they returned, the girl's appearance was totally different. The rash had cleared up, she was putting on weight, and she was definitely on the road to recovery. After the third visit the girl had completely recovered.

It was only after the incident that a thought occurred to me. They had mentioned that the girl's problem was that her immune system had broken down. It struck me that this was very similar to AIDS. I wrote a letter to the doctor in charge of the AIDS section of James Hospital in Dublin, explaining about myself and the case, and asking for permission to treat ten people with full-blown AIDS at no cost to anyone. I received a reply saying they received requests from all kinds of people from the alternative medicine field but they always refused. They didn't consider that what I did could be of any advantage to people with AIDS. I contacted some AIDS groups in Dublin, but they also turned down the offer.

The *Sunday World*, however, did an item about the incident and my interest in AIDS, and as a result a Dublin family contacted me. Their son was in St Michael's Hospital suffering from an AIDS-related illness, and they asked me to treat him. When I first saw him, he was wasting away and lay on the bed only half conscious. When I returned the following week he was sitting up in bed.

"I wish to hell I could get out of this bleedin' place," he said, and I knew he was recovering. Two months later, he visited my home to thank me.

I saw a man in America who was dying through the AIDS virus. When I visited him he was in what the patients termed "Death Row" – people with full-blown AIDS were there waiting to die. The last time I saw him, after treatment, he was walking six miles a day, enjoying mountain-climbing, and back to a normal diet and healthy life. I asked him if he would get a blood test to see if the disease had actually gone.

"If I went back looking for a blood test to see if I still had the AIDS virus," he said, "they'd probably send me off for psychiatric treatment."

I saw a man in Montreal with AIDS in 1990. He was brought to me in a wheelchair, and looked so ill that if he'd died before my eyes I wouldn't have been surprised. Long after I'd treated him, I got a phone call from another man with AIDS in Montreal, telling me the man I'd treated was back at work. I've treated three people with AIDS, and to the best of my knowledge two are now well and living normal lives – the Dublin man relapsed with another illness his immune system couldn't fight. While the cures and remission seem extraordinary, I have learned never to try predicting the outcome of my treatment. Simple things can fail while major illnesses can be cured.

I think sometimes of giving up this work. I've always been a healer, and I don't know any other life. But apart from healing, my hands are useless. I've never been good at DIY, and I seem to have no flair for any kind of handiwork. It seems my hands are meant to heal and nothing else. I often feel ashamed of what I am and what I do. I sometimes hide what I do because I feel like an oddball, and if at all possible I'll avoid telling people about myself. Recently, during my work in Glasgow, a taxi-driver taking me from the airport asked me what line of work I was in. I said I was in advertising, because I didn't want to face his reaction if I told him I was a healer.

I'd never recommend what I do for a living to anyone else; I certainly hope none of my family ever get into it – especially my children. There's a danger that some might put pressure on my eldest, as the first son of a seventh son, to go into healing. I hope he doesn't.

In fact, I'm sorry in some ways that my career is healing because it does affect my life a great deal. Most of the time I sit in a hotel after my clinics, scared to say what I do because I either end up getting asked to heal somebody or I get insulted. Sometimes I think there must be some kind of divine inspiration coming to me to keep me going at it in spite of all this, because I always feel that I stick out like a sore thumb in company. I'm expected to be different, when all I want is to be treated normally. The other side of the coin, as I keep reminding myself and as I always try to point out to others, is that people do get healed.

I'm sorry, too, that my life has been hounded by a pre-occupation in the media about money. I live well, and I believe I earn what I have. Over the years very many people have come to my clinics, been treated, and paid nothing. In the early days, the tax man didn't believe this. Certainly, the media made great mileage out of the idea that I had money pouring into my hands. I've always made it clear that the person who gives me a hundred pounds and the person who gives me nothing both stand the same chance of being cured. I don't sell my healing as it's not mine to sell.

Keeping a record of the cures is my own self-defence mechanism. No one can ever call me a fraud. I have lists and lists of people who have been healed and are prepared to have their stories told publicly. Anyone is welcome to investigate the claims. They are totally legitimate, and my own conscience is clear on this matter. No one can ever say I don't cure people.

It's possible that people will start associating me with new-age and alternative medicine and might shed some of their scepticism. Certainly, the attitude of the medical profession is changing. In recent times, four doctors have come to my clinic to be treated. As I said to one of them, the times they are a-changing. I've survived the cynicism and the scepticism and the abuse. I've never overstretched claims of my ability to heal, but maybe at last there are more people open to accepting the one simple truth which has shaped my life for better or for worse: I have healing powers.

I very rarely get letters from people who have been cured, even though I would be very grateful to hear from them. Usually I hear of cures through people who have come to the clinics because they know someone who has been cured by me. Another way is when I've cured someone of a complaint years before and they've come back with a different complaint, seeking to be healed again.

For better or worse, I've spent my life as a healer. It's work I was literally born to do and I'll keep on doing it. I believe people will continue to come to me because they know they have good reason for believing I represent a real possibility of relief from illnesses, even though the healing can't be explained.

TEN

I have been a healer in a full-time professional capacity since the age of seventeen and over the past two decades my ideas about healing have changed and developed. Although I know my healing is very simple and unsophisticated – all I do is put my right hand on the affected part of the person who comes to me – stories of people with healing powers predate the development of conventional medicine, and I have seen the results of my own gift.

I think I have healing powers because I was brought up believing that I could heal. It was bred into me without a question of doubt. My powers were brought out in a natural way, and I believe the same thing could have happened to anybody – be it first, sixth or whatever son or daughter. It was instilled into me that there was simply no way I could not heal,

137

and because I started at a subconscious level as a child I believe my healing has developed naturally. I learned healing as fluently and completely as I learned to walk and talk. It was accepted as being something I could do, and so the gift developed fully instead of being left unused as I suspect is the case with other people.

I've been called a faith-healer all my life and the more I try to escape that tag the more, it seems, I'm given it. There are so many things that prove it wrong – treating animals is one example. Recently, in Scotland, I cured a dog of cancer. The story was featured in a newspaper, showing a photograph of me holding the dog. A man came up to me the following day and said, "Aren't you the faith-healer who cured the dog?"

I remember one striking refutal of the "faith-healer" claim. A woman came to me suffering from psoriasis all over her body. She was very embarrassed about being treated by me, and she would only allow me to touch certain affected parts. Two months later, she came back to me. To her surprise her condition had been completely cured in the areas I'd touched but remained as bad as ever on the rest of her body.

Another of the many disproofs is a trend in the way people respond to my healing. Many get worse before they get better. I believe that this is the disease working its way out. Surely if something was a faith cure it would be all in a person's mind and they would feel better straight away. I tend to believe that the worse the initial reaction, the stronger the cure – although this is by no means always the case. Some cures happen without any reaction to me or any initial adverse effects on the patient.

I feel more comfortable in the company of people who are sceptical about what I do than with those who have very strong faith in it. That way, I'm never bothered about it or asked questions: if people don't believe in what I do, they leave me alone. Those who believe in me want to talk endlessly about

FINBARR NOLAN

it, and I get enough of all that when I'm in my clinic. Once I'm outside the clinic I like to get away from the healing and get on with my life.

Brendan was very enthusiastic about what I did and he could never understand my failures. He had a theory that I had an energy that operated with people. He believed that when someone was ill, it was as though they needed to be charged up with healing energy and that I carried that energy. He claimed that when it worked it was because my energy was compatible with the ill person. When treatment was unsuccessful, on the other hand, it was as a result of my energy being incompatible.

I touch the affected area of the patient's body, and there's no pressure in my touch and no effort on my part to think of the person being treated. My mind is vacant; I could be thinking about a football game I've seen, or how many people are in the clinic or whatever. Even at the start I wasn't conscious of healing. I remember I had a schoolfriend who used to help me in clinics, carrying the holy-water bowl that I would dip my fingers into as I treated people. This boy was a joker who used to nudge me as I worked and point out some pretty girl down the queue and we would giggle.

I also know that I have no control over what I do. For that reason alone I believe that what I do comes from God. If the gift came from me then I'd have control over it. I believe that anything that's natural in this world comes from God. That's my reason for believing that what I do is totally natural and that what I do should be called 'natural healing'.

I can never guarantee that the healing will work. If I could tell someone with absolute certainty that I could cure them, then the power would be mine and I might be tempted to abuse it for my own gain. I have been reminded time and time again, however, that the healing is not mine to give. There might be times when I'm exhausted or ill and the healing works. Similarly, there are times when I'm in an exceptional frame of mind and feeling full of life and the healing doesn't work. I've had success with animals; I've had success with children – even newborn babies; I've had success with people in comas; sceptics have been healed by me: yet I am forever being labelled a con man or a faith-healer.

My powers have never been tested in Ireland. The problem seems to be that if anyone carries out scientific experiments on me, I will be the only one to gain. If what I do could be put into tablet-form, it would sell all over the world and plenty of people would want to test it. I have often been sent strips of cloth and asked to touch the material and return it to the ill person. Again, I don't feel this is the correct way to use the gift – I have to treat the patient in person.

When people come to my clinics I have a standard speech. I tell them I have to touch the bare skin of the affected parts with my right hand. I have to see them on three separate days. I tell them that if they are taking any prescribed medication they should continue to do so. I warn them of the possibility that they might initially experience an adverse reaction to my treatment, though normally such a reaction is a good sign. I then ask if people have been with me before or if they know anyone who has been with me before, and it usually turns out from this that I can find out about cures.

I don't know whether or not a person is cured for about six months after I've treated them. Sometimes people come to me and get better for a few days but then suffer a relapse. The only sure way I have of knowing someone is cured is to contact them six months afterwards to find out how they are. My healing takes time.

A lot of people come to me expecting to walk out the door cured, but it really doesn't work like that. Media people, too, come to my clinics expecting to witness instant cures. I've often seen people cured after one visit, but a month later they relapse. It takes time to know – I have to be patient, and the people who come to me have to be patient. Most results happen six weeks after the third visit. I encourage people not to dismiss hopes of getting a cure until they've allowed this period of time to elapse. For my part, I never consider a cure as genuine unless people remain significantly better for a lengthy period after the treatment. I don't put any significance in people coming back to me a day or two after being treated saying they feel better.

Sceptics often say that the people I treat successfully are only cured for a while. I accept that this can be the case sometimes, but on the other hand many of my cures date back over twenty years now, without recurrence.

I feel that if someone has an ailment and comes to me before going on to medication or undergoing surgery then my healing stands a better chance. I think the natural healing has a better chance to work under such circumstances.

People come to me three times – in the name of the Father, the Son, and the Holy Ghost. As mentioned earlier, this is one tradition that I don't feel I should break with. Also, I have very rarely seen instances where people are fully cured after one or two visits, even though recovery might start after the initial treatment.

One man with an ailment came to me three times in Cavan in 1971 but wasn't cured. He came to me again three times in Cashel in 1978, but without success. Then he visited me three times in Cork in 1982 and he was finally cured. It again goes to show that in what I do there are a lot of questions and not too many answers.

A fair amount of people I treat get worse before they get better. If they're in intense pain with arthritis, for example, they will commonly feel the pain even more severely for a while. To my mind, this is the illness working its way out of the system by burning itself out. Another common reaction is that the pain might change position slightly, which is usually a good indication that the ailment is moving out of the body.

I usually see patients in groups, and a lot of people don't like that. In my opinion, though, it's good for people to see others who are also ill – it can be an eye-opener for them to see the suffering that goes on and may help them get their own illness into perspective. Apart from that, people can feel reassured with others around them.

I would never ask anyone if they wanted to be healed. They must come to me. In the early days, people approached me in public – in a bar or a restaurant, for example – asking for treatment, and on a few occasions I agreed. But I don't think it's the right way to approach my work and I won't do that anymore. When people ask me now, I just tell them where I'm holding my clinics and if they want to come along, that's fine.

Most doctors are either silent about what I do or object to it. I treated a woman in Dundalk who had tuberculosis and she was cured completely. She had been attending hospital for her condition, and she went to the doctor to tell him that she had been to see me and was completely cured. The doctor simply burst out laughing. The woman later told me about this incident and I assured her that she had the last laugh.

Whenever I'm ill, I go to my doctor. My relationship with those who have treated me has been very good, and I have many witty exchanges with the family doctor.

I've never studied medicine. I have a basic knowledge of complaints so that I know where to touch for various illnesses and conditions. It's possible that there have been times when I have touched the wrong place when treating a patient and perhaps missed an opportunity for my healing to work.

Patients have sometimes come to me with X-rays or with letters from their doctor to hospitals as a way of being specific about their ailment.

The restrictions on my freedom to hold clinics stem mostly from the fact that I have no medical qualifications, and if a qualified doctor were willing to work with me I would be free to practise my healing almost everywhere in the world. It seems unlikely, though, that any doctor would ever agree to such an approach. As I discovered at my Greek clinic, it must be galling to study for years to enter the medical profession and then come across someone who has a natural ability to heal.

The report by Dr Willner at the end of this book tells of an experiment in which he, an ordinary general practitioner, had me treat (without their knowledge) ten patients he couldn't cure. While I can't imagine it happening, I'd be perfectly happy to go to the clinic of any doctor who presented me with such a situation – after all, as I've said before, most of the people I deal with are people the medical profession has failed to help. What I'd love to see happening – though I don't suppose I ever will – would be for me to go into a hospital and have a room there where people could come to me if they wanted to or doctors would give me medical histories of patients and explain where exactly the treatment would be most effective. I'm used to being the last resort for people who are suffering with illnesses. I'd be much happier if my healing gift were treated as a resource for people right from the outset rather than be presented – by patients, media and medical profession alike – as a fringe choice made in desperation.

I have learned down the years to treat certain illnesses in other ways than those I'd previously imagined. Most noticeable are the results I get since I changed my approach to treating depression. I used to treat depression by touching the sufferer's head. Now, I see it as being more a chemical or physical imbalance and I touch other areas of the body – for example the liver, the pancreas, the colon, the bowel, the heart and the thyroid gland. I've noticed a dramatic improvement in results since making this change.

One of the most interesting developments for me recently has been my work with the American John Grinder. He is a leader in the new field of study called Neuro Linguistic Programming. It is part of a system devised to explore people in a psychic way to learn how we behave, and how behaviour alters personality and abilities. The idea behind NLP is that those who studied me carefully enough would be able to follow the same path of behaviour and would also be able to heal. John has used me as the basis for several seminars where participants study me and the way I work. The aim was for them to follow my model and through that discover healing powers in themselves. There would up to a hundred partic-ipants at these seminars, watching me as I treated patients and examining the details of how I went about the process. The way I stood, the way I looked, the way I dealt with people – everything was studied closely.

The last such seminar I attended was in Heidelburg in Germany. There were 150 people there who wanted to be healers. It was the first time I'd been in Germany since my experience of being imprisoned for healing. When the seminar was over I went out for a meal with the organisers. The women who ran the seminar mentioned over the meal that twenty-six of those attending the seminar were doctors. I burst out laughing: after all the hassle I'd had years before in Germany, and all the condemnation I'd had from doctors, it was staggering to realise that the medical profession was coming round to the point where they wanted to learn about my kind of healing. The young doctors coming to study me were disillusioned with medicine as they had studied it and believed there was something worth exploring in my work.

In one of the seminars with John Grinder, people touched my head as I sat with my eyes covered. I was asked if any of them felt different from the rest. I identified one person as having the same kind of touch that people had often told me I had when healing them – she was Linda Shapiro. She has since gone on to carry out her own healing of many people.

Linda's way of discovering her touch healing through studying me involved some interesting measures. She first imagined and believed an incident before her birth where it was decided that she would be a healer. She then mimicked gestures of mine when healing, including a twitching of the upper lip which she noticed. She is very aware of the fact that her hand is hot when she heals and she can often sense vibrations between herself and her patient. She also feels that she must wish to heal that which is meant to be healed and has found that the faith of the patient isn't necessary for successful treatment. Linda believes that the healing is a universal energy working through her and that lack of ego and lack of rational thought is required when healing.

While I never consciously aimed at any of these things, I can recognise all of Linda's discoveries as part of my own experience as a healer. I am delighted to have been a part of her being opened up to her gift, and I am grateful for the ways in which her studies have thrown some light on my own experiences.

Through NLP I also met Herb Lustig. He is a child psychologist from Philadelphia who incorporates hypnotism into his work. He felt that he had healing powers and wanted to study me. He came to Ireland to watch how I worked, and he said that he believed that while I was treating people they showed signs of going into a brief hypnotic state. I have no idea if that is so – but it was his observation.

A person comes to me and I touch them. Even if it doesn't do them any good, it certainly won't do them any harm. I once asked a group of about fifteen people in a clinic how my hands felt when I'd treated them. Six said they felt my hands very hot, and the rest said my hands didn't feel any different from a normal touch. I suspect there is significance in those who feel heat in my hands.

I've noticed over the years that my right hand, my healing hand, has never been damaged. It rarely even suffers minor problems such as cuts or bruises. One instance in particular made a deep impression on me. Even though my healing has always worked independent of my own health, it seems my right hand is in some way affected by the healing it channels to others. In 1973 I was sitting in the back of an Audi car. In that particular model, the battery was under the back seat. I was coming home with a friend, and the back seat slipped and my right hand went down on top of the battery. It was very severely burned by the acid. My friend rushed me to a nearby hospital. They treated the burns with ointments and bandaged up my hand. They were going to keep me in overnight, but I didn't want to stay. I went home instead, and fell into bed.

The next day the same friend called around to see how I was. I had slept late, and when he woke me, I realised that my hand felt fine. I unravelled the bandage, and to my amazement there wasn't a mark on my hand. All sign of the burn had disappeared completely.

Some local people around Cavan believed that most diseases were caused by worms and that the gift of the seventh son of a seventh son was the ability to kill the worms. This probably stems back to biblical ideas of the body being made of clay – "dust thou art and to dust thou shalt return". Those were the kind of superstitions that grew up around me in the early days.

At this stage in my life, however, I have grave doubts about the legend of the seventh son of a seventh son. In my family there were seven boys. But in my father's family there were thirteen children – six girls and seven boys. Even though in one sense my father was a seventh son, the intermingling of boys and girls casts a certain amount of doubt on the claim. It was only when healing became my livelihood that I was acknowledged as the seventh son of a seventh son.

Nowadays I don't know what to make of the whole thing. I find it hard to believe that just because of an accident of birth I can have healing powers. It has also been a problem in foreign countries because the legend means nothing outside of Ireland and a few other Celtic areas. Irish travelling people have a strong tradition of believing in the myth of the seventh son of a seventh son. I remember once, when I was working in Castlebar, a group of travellers came to my hotel asking to see "the priest". I sometimes wish the label had never been put on me, though it's possible then that my healing powers would never have been found and developed.

I remember once going to the editor of a Dutch newspaper seeking some publicity and he asked me how I could heal. I explained that I was the seventh son of a seventh son and his reaction was to say: "I'm the first son of a first son – what can I do?"

I'm sure that many people have healing powers. The extent of that ability might vary, but at the end of the day I suspect we all have healing powers and that some happen to be better at healing just as some happen to be better at football or whatever other talent. There are probably people who can heal better than I, yet who have never discovered that talent in themselves. I'm sure that I became competent as a healer because it was accepted and developed in me from the time of the first cure when I was two-and-a-half years old.

The attitude towards my healing has changed dramatically over the past few years. I gave a radio show for the BBC in

Belfast and a doctor from Stratford-on-Avon was brought in to present the other side of the argument – but he turned out to have more belief in healing than even I do. The turnaround in opinions has been extraordinary.

The ability to heal is a real power. I have it. Others have it. There is much, much more to be learned about it, and in my own clumsy way I have gathered ideas over the years. There's yet to be a comprehensive study of the phenomenon, but the studies that have been done on me are presented in a following chapter. I would never shy away from submitting to tests, and I would never claim to know all the answers.

I find it very disheartening when people I have cured won't allow their stories to be used for publicity. Without results, I don't exist, and I believe that if people with ailments were to read that I had cured someone else of the same illness it might give them heart. It's frustrating to have people thinking I'm a fraud while at the same time I'm aware of cures that I can't tell anyone about. There may well be times when people require confidentiality, but in the majority of cases I can't see why people won't agree to their stories being told. In the following chapter, ten stories of cures are given. I'm grateful to these people for agreeing to have their cases included in my book, and I hope the reader will find the accounts interesting.

I can be called a fake or a fraud because there are lots of people who come to me and don't get healed. Then again, there are many people I have healed. For the thousands I haven't healed, there are thousands I have healed. I can't control the gift and I don't know why. But I don't pretend to control it, and I'm honest in saying that I have healing powers. The cases are there and the proof is clear. People can believe what they want to believe, but I know in my own heart and conscience that I heal people and I will continue with my work as long as people come to me. Even if I don't have all the answers, I at least have the certainty that I have healed and I have a gift which people can benefit from.

Looking back over the years since the whole adventure of becoming a well-known healer began, I can't be the judge of how well I handled the gift or my life. If there were times when greed or stupidity got the better of me then I can only trust that such things are in the past. The aim I seek above all now, and one of my main reasons for writing this book, is to have what I do taken seriously. I'm willing to be studied, to have cases examined, to have theories tested. Maybe, though, none of the mysteries of the gift will be explained. Being a healer doesn't make me wise and it also doesn't make me insensitive to the sceptics. I want my healing to be acknowledged, even if it doesn't fit in with modern medicine. And I've wanted for a long time to tell the story of what it was like to have my fate decided the day I was born and my life shaped by a gift I neither understand nor control.

TEN CURES

When Finbarr worked with me on this book, he particularly wanted to include stories of people healed by him. When we came to the point of selecting those to interview, his attitude was typically open. He sat down with me and opened a folder bulging with pages and pages of names of people who had been healed. There were a few stories he recommended – such as that of Anthony Milligan – but the rest I was free to choose at random.

All the people I spoke to had one thing in common – they like Finbarr. Their experience of going to him was one they found calming and positive. Whether they went to him when he was a young boy or in recent years, all the people I spoke to remember him with admiration and fondness. Even if he has no medical qualifications, he could certainly teach many doctors about the notion of "bedside manners".

Their stories are an intriguing insight into just how remarkable a gift Finbarr has.

Martin Duffy

ANTHONY MILLIGAN

Edendariff, Ballinahinch, County Down

In early 1978, Anthony Milligan began suffering from very severe pains in his stomach. He eventually went to his doctor, who in turn sent him to Lagan Valley Hospital for tests and X-rays.

"I remember every bump in the road," Anthony says, "the pain I got from the jolting of the car was so bad."

As the illness worsened he was put on more and more pain-killers until he was taking one an hour. Sleep was impossible, and Anthony, living alone, would get up in the middle of the night and go for walks in an attempt to take his mind off the pain. He was losing weight drastically, and ultimately dropped to seven stone. He was told that he was too ill to live alone, and became a lodger in a new home.

He was sent for more tests, and a decision was made to carry out an exploratory operation. As he lay in the hospital bed waiting for the operation, a doctor came to him.

"Tell me," the doctor asked, "how many bottles of whiskey do you drink a day?"

Anthony was shocked. He was more likely to be able to tell him how many glasses he drank in a year.

"What you have is a whiskey drinker's disease," the doctor explained. The exploratory operation involved taking a sample from the pancreas to run tests. After the operation, Anthony's blood pressure dropped and he had to be taken into a private ward and treated for days before the pressure returned to normal. Unknown to him at the time, the doctors had told his sisters that he had only six weeks to live. Anthony had cancer of the pancreas.

His sisters brought Anthony home to die, and in the following weeks his pain grew more and more intense. The bed sheets had to be changed three times a day because of the sweat pouring from him. He walked the floor night after night. He was taking the strong drug Diconal to ease the pain but that had ceased to have any effect. His doctor then began injecting him with morphine, but as this involved a visit by the doctor every four hours, Anthony asked him not to go to so much inconvenience. The doctor put him on morphine and brandy.

"That's not a very tasteful mouthful I can assure you. It's like poison," Anthony told me. What he didn't realise was that by being prescribed addictive drugs he was being treated as terminally ill.

Anthony asked his doctor if the surgeon who had carried out the operation could visit him. When he came, Anthony wanted the surgeon to say straight out that he had cancer, but the man had been asked by the sisters not to say this and so he declined. His surgeon wanted Anthony to go back to the hospital to be cared for, but Anthony wanted to spend his last days at home.

His sisters announced to Anthony one night that they were taking him into the nearby town of Ballinahinch. Finbarr Nolan was doing a clinic there, and they wanted Anthony to be treated by him. Anthony had never even heard of Finbarr Nolan, but through his sisters' insistence he suffered the painful car journey into town. There were crowds at the clinic, and Anthony was in such pain that he pleaded with his sisters to take him home. That night was as bad as those before, and from early in the morning Anthony sat on the wall outside his house trying to take his mind off the pain.

A car pulled up outside the house and one of Anthony's neighbours climbed out of the passenger seat.

"Do you recognise the man driving the car?" she asked.

Anthony didn't.

"That's the man you were hoping to see last night – that's Finbarr Nolan."

Fate works in curious ways. This neighbour had caused Anthony to get into a minor spot of trouble long before when he was working in the local bar. As her way of making amends, she had gone to Finbarr and asked him to make this special trip.

Finbarr went into the house with Anthony and treated him.

"He touched me around the stomach and the back," Anthony said. "I thought his hands were on fire."

As Finbarr drove away, he turned to the woman and said he thought there was no hope for Anthony Milligan. But that night, for the first time in many months, Anthony enjoyed a good night's sleep.

Finbarr made his three visits within little more than a week, and Anthony began recovering. He was later taken to Belfast for tests with new advanced equipment and he was told that he didn't have cancer. For Anthony, it was proof that Finbarr had cured him. For the doctors, it was their basis for claiming that he had been diagnosed incorrectly in the first place – although they never offered an opinion on what they then believed he had suffered from or how he had been cured. They even suggested that the exploratory operation had cured him, despite the fact that his condition had continued to deteriorate after it.

Anthony's recovery was extraordinary. He was soon putting on weight again. The pain was gone, and his health was restored. He naturally became a great advocate of Finbarr. He once referred to Finbarr a man whose son was deaf – and the boy was cured.

Four years after his cure, Anthony was bringing a couple to one of Finbarr's clinics and as he walked across the ballroom floor he saw the shocked expression on Finbarr's face as the healer recognised the transformed man.

"Don't tell me," Finbarr said. "Don't tell me – Anthony Milligan? Well, you're one man I never expected to see in my life again!"

Anthony laughs as he recounts that moment. "Finbarr kept saying 'I don't believe it, I don't believe it.' He was as much surprised as I was by the cure."

Anthony's recovery made a very strong impression on Finbarr. "I don't often remember the people I see, but I remember very well going out to see Anthony. As I was driving away after treating him, I told the woman who had brought me that I didn't believe I'd see Anthony again. On my second visit to him, Anthony told me that the pain in his pancreas had gone. I didn't make any comment, because some people who come to me get better for a while and then relapse. Even after the third visit, I still felt that Anthony was fatally ill.

"When I saw him that night at my clinic, it was as if I was watching the dead arise. Years later, in 1985, I was holding a clinic in Downpatrick and a number of people came to me saying they knew Anthony and knew I had cured him. As he had so often brought people to me or recommended me to people, I decided to visit and thank him.

"I was told at my first visit not to tell him he had cancer. When finally we talked in 1985 about the case he said he found out afterwards that he'd been suffering from that disease."

His family remember that as Anthony was starting to feel better, he decided one day in Downpatrick to renew his driver's licence and walked up a steep hill instead of having them bring him in the car. When he managed the trip they were convinced that he was cured and back in good health.

"Anthony was known as 'the walking dead' because the people around felt he was surely going to die when he had cancer," Finbar told me. "I have remained friends with Anthony, and seeing him today is a great antidote for me when I'm constantly being faced with disbelief and scepticism. Seeing him gives my confidence in my healing a great boost."

STEPHANIE CARROLL

Mourne Road, Drimnagh, Dublin 12

Stephanie is a ballroom dancer and along with her strong dress sense goes a pride in her appearance. Twenty-one years ago when she suffered rheumatic lumps on her legs, therefore, she was desperate to treat the problem. Standard medical treatment cleared all but one of the lumps – but that one grew large and unsightly and very painful. "The pain was unbearable," she said. "I could hardly walk, and I was so bad the doctor suggested I get a stick." She was attending Hume Street Hospital for treatment of the condition and they had told her that her leg was in an acute state. They were dressing the lump but it wasn't responding to any treatment. It was particularly painful at night because the blankets would rub against it. "I was in agony – I couldn't sleep," she said.

Stephanie heard of Finbarr at the time he was based in Balgriffin on the north county side of Dublin. She had two young children and no transport, and the journey out to his clinic was a difficult one to plan. She didn't know of anyone who'd been treated by him, but she believed in healing and felt that Finbarr would be able to cure her.

One day she left her son in school and set off on the bus journey into town and across to Balgriffin with her baby daughter. When she found the hall where Finbarr was holding the clinic there were crowds waiting for him. When it came to Stephanie's turn to be treated he laid his right hand on her leg and Stephanie also prayed to be healed.

156

Finbarr told Stephanie that she would have to come three times, and warned her that her condition might get worse before getting better. By the second visit, Stephanie was indeed much worse and was limping badly. The lump was weeping and was extremely painful.

On the third visit, however, events took a very dramatic turn. Before her eyes, the lump on Stephanie's leg started shrinking and fading away. "My leg is healed," she announced to Finbarr, and he turned to the rest of the people present and asked if anyone else had been healed. Several people stood up. Stephanie was so delighted with her cure that she went around telling family and friends. When she went back to the hospital they couldn't believe the change – but she didn't tell them she had been to Finbarr.

Stephanie had great belief in Finbarr and later wanted to go to him about another problem but by then he had left Ireland on his travels.

In 1990 Stephanie was suffering from eczema on the same leg and by then she knew that Finbarr held clinics in his home. She went to Finbarr three times and was cured – though the problem still returns to a lesser extent. During her visits Stephanie also met a man who told her that Finbarr had healed the back problem from which he had suffered for years after falling off a ladder.

Stephanie has a very strong belief in healing as an act of faith and is certain that the healing comes from God. She believes that everyone has healing hands if they trust in God and pray to Him. "It's really God that heals through people. I think you must believe in God and really want to be healed," she said, and added that she could feel the power of the healing in Finbarr's hand. "It felt like a vibration – a pins-and-needles sensation. I could feel the healing every time I went to Finbarr."

VINCENT GERAGHTY

Moatfield Park, Dublin 5

Many people suffer pain in their back and there are many alternative methods of treating the ordeal of backache. Vincent Geraghty didn't know exactly how he hurt his back, but he knew all about the agony of the consequences. He was always prone to pain in his lower back, possibly due to his height, and on this occasion he was suffering badly.

"I couldn't sit, I couldn't lie down," he said. "I used to lie on my stomach on the floor watching television, and then my children would have to roll me across the floor to slowly lift myself up by the chair – it was that bad."

Vincent went to his doctor, who referred him to a specialist. The earliest appointment he could get, however, was three months away. Vincent was out of work and in extreme pain and had no wish to wait that length of time.

The first treatment he tried in the meantime was to go to an osteopath. Vincent laughed as he remembered: "He twisted me this way and that way – I wasn't able to walk out of the place," he said.

Vincent then saw an advertisement for Finbarr and went to a clinic in his home. A native of Westmeath, Vincent had been cured in his teens of ringworm on his leg by a seventh son known in the area. Vincent believed that Finbarr could help him, and he went to the clinic very much wanting the healing to work.

"The first time I went to Finbarr, after the treatment I couldn't get out of the chair and he had to help me up," Vincent said.

He went to Finbarr three times in the same week, and by the third visit the pain was fading away. "I didn't really notice it going away. I just realised I was in great form and not a bother on me. I really do believe that Finbarr cured me: I have no doubts about that."

I asked him if, as is sometimes the case, he felt worse before he felt better. Again he broke into a warm laugh. "The state I was in, I couldn't have felt any worse," he said. "The only thing I could do was improve."

All trouble had long gone by the time the appointment with the specialist came around. "He examined me inside out and couldn't find anything wrong. All the explanation he could give was that I possibly put out a disc and it went back in again."

That incident happened twenty years ago, and since then Vincent has had very little trouble with his back. "Sometimes it feels stiff, but that could be old age. I'm sixty-seven now," he says. "But I have great sympathy for anyone who says they have trouble with their back. I never experienced a pain like it before or since."

Talking about the seventh son who had treated him in his teens, Vincent mentioned that the man was later said to have lost his gift because he charged a fee to treat a wealthy woman. The woman wasn't cured and had to go to another healer who didn't ask for any money.

"Finbarr, of course, has to make his living by what he does, but he didn't mention a fee to me and I gave him my donation," Vincent concluded. "He does a lot of good for a lot of people and I found him to be a nice, warm man."

159

PAULA MATTHEWS

Summerhill Place, Twinbrook, Belfast

Paula Matthews was the youngest of eight children. From the time she was born, she took convulsive fits. A cycle quickly emerged where the ill child would be allowed home from the hospital, would take another fit, and would have to return to hospital. For the first two years of her life, Paula rarely spent a full week at home. She was given many tests in hospital, and was being treated with phenabarbitone. Finally her parents were told by two doctors in the hospital that Paula was suffering from epilepsy.

"The hospital told us that she was an epileptic and would be for the rest of her life," her mother said. "They talked to us about what to expect for her life – that she wouldn't die, but that as she grew older she might take a fit at any time. She might collapse in the street."

Her father learned to help Paula through the fits, but always she would come out of them in such a weakened state that she had to be taken to hospital.

Mrs Matthews heard that Finbarr Nolan was holding a clinic in Aghalee, near Belfast, and she brought her child. After the first visit, Paula had another fit. It wasn't as extreme as her usual fits, and her father helped her through it without needing to take her to hospital. It was the last she ever had. Paula is now twenty-one years old and has enjoyed good health all her life since.

Her parents went back to the doctors, telling them that Finbarr had cured their daughter. The doctors refused to accept this, and the consequences of this have been curious. Whenever the grown family have had children of their own, they would be asked before inoculations if any member of the family had suffered from such illnesses as epilepsy. The parents would say that their sister had epilepsy and the children would be treated in that light – yet no doctor ever confirmed that Paula had been cured or denied that she had epilepsy.

Obviously, curing a two-year-old child doesn't involve faith-healing. The case is remarkable in the speed and completeness of the cure and in the fact that Finbarr cured an infant who could have had no idea of what was happening. Also, the rejection by doctors of the plain facts before them gives some idea of the disregard with which Finbarr's work is viewed by some members of the medical profession.

WILLIAM LEWIS

Church Gardens, Rathmines, Dublin

William Lewis retired recently from his job as a driver at the age of sixty-seven. He is a robust man. His wife, Bridie, says he's never sick. Twenty-two years ago, when they had five young children to raise, the story was very different. Bill developed rheumatoid arthritis in his early forties. It began one day with a pain in his foot, which his doctor treated first as a possible sprain or muscle strain. The problem became worse, however, and worked its way through his body. The doctor diagnosed rheumatoid arthritis, and explained that it was a hereditary illness. Soon Bill had to wear a strap on his arm at all times and his joints became more and more painful.

"If I'd had a hatchet I'd have chopped them off," he says to me, extending his fingers. "I used to cry with the pain."

The arthritis was so bad that he couldn't bend his fingers. He had sleepless nights and his day would begin in agony, rolling himself out of bed. It would take him over half an hour to loosen up. His joints were badly swollen, and two six-week sessions of physiotherapy brought him little relief. He had the condition for four years and all the while it was growing steadily worse.

Bill feared he was going to become a cripple. He saw people in physiotherapy with the condition in a more advanced state, and he was considering going to Lourdes in the hope of a cure.

Bridie's grandfather came from Gowna and she was born in a little town not far from there. She knew the Nolan family:

Mrs Nolan was well known in the area as a pianist and for her work for the church; Sergeant Nolan was considered a gentleman. In her youth, Bridie had heard of Finbarr's birth and that farmers were bringing their animals to him.

Bridie and Bill were on holidays in Cavan when Finbarr was holding his clinics in Arvagh. This was at the height of his new fame, when thousands were going to him. One of their friends, Eddie McCann, had been to Finbarr and urged Bill to go. Bridie encouraged Bill too. Each visit took a day, the crowds were so huge. The treatment itself took a very short time.

Bill remembers Finbarr as a pleasant lad at the centre of this extraordinary spectacle. Bill told him about the arthritis throughout his body, and Finbarr moved his hands up along his body, lightly touching Bill's joints. Bill felt no strong sensation when Finbarr treated him. He felt relief, but didn't notice anything unusual in the young man's touch. Finbarr told him to continue with his hospital treatment, but a week after the third visit, Bill was completely free from pain. The swelling had gone, and he no longer went for hospital treatment.

"I haven't looked back since," Bill says. "I haven't had a pain or an ache – the arthritis is completely gone."

People at work were commenting on how well Bill looked and he told them he'd been to Finbarr. He stopped wearing his arm strap, and he had full movement in all his joints.

Bill has no doubt that he was cured by Finbarr. The hospital treatments and medication had given only brief respite from the pain, whereas after Finbarr's treatment the condition disappeared.

"Finbarr is very genuine." Bill says. "He doesn't claim to cure anyone – it's the people themselves who say they've been cured. I think the hand of God works through Finbarr. He has a great gift, and he makes it clear that he has no control over it. Some people say that if you've been cured by Finbarr it's because your illness was all in the mind. But if you've cancer or arthritis or a tumour it's in your body, it's not in your mind. My brother has the same condition I had, but he never went to Finbarr and he's never had relief."

"I knew Finbarr to be a seventh son, though I didn't know if he was the seventh son of a seventh son," Bridie adds. "Some say that arthritis is caused by a worm in the system – that might be just a superstition – and a seventh son is said to be able to kill the worms. But if God grants the gift that's all that matters. Bill is a different man since the cure."

MURIEL BOWEN

Annalong, Kilkeel, County Down

Muriel Bowen and her husband Bill run an excellent restaurant together. She was an air hostess, and is a vivacious woman who lives a healthy and active life. Muriel and Bill are very positive people, and when Muriel was first informed of the fact that she had cancer they shared an absolute determination to beat the challenge. When the doctor broke the news, Bill promised that Muriel and he would treat the doctor to a bottle of champagne at their restaurant five years later. The doctor wasn't in any way optimistic.

Muriel had been suffering continuous bleeding, and her doctor referred her for tests which led to a radical hysterectomy with the aim of removing the cancer. It was discovered, however, that the cancer had entered her lymph glands and so was spreading through her body. Her youth and health, ironically, meant that the disease spread all the more rapidly. The problem was so extreme that even radiation treatment wasn't feasible.

She was allowed home and was brought back for tests three weeks later, but subsequently discovered that the hospital didn't expect her to live until her next check-up three weeks after. Muriel never felt very ill, even though the tests clearly showed that the cancer was out of control. As the weeks passed, Muriel and Bill decided that if the medical profession weren't able to help, then they had to turn elsewhere. They had seen

Finbarr on a television show, and they had been impressed by him. They then sought him out, and Muriel drove to Dublin with a friend for a weekend.

"In a sense it was an act of rebellion – a refusal to give in," Muriel says. "When I went to Finbarr there was no hocus pocus and he was very gentle and unassuming. I liked that about him and I think it's brave of him not to pretend to know how it works or if it will work."

Muriel remembers Finbarr's warning that sometimes people take a bad initial reaction to treatment. His touch felt in no way unusual to her, however, and she experienced no strong reaction.

Driving home on Sunday after the third session, Muriel felt a very warm sensation rise through her body. "It felt like a burning sensation," she says, "but it only lasted a few minutes."

Muriel was still going for the check-ups, and was referred to another hospital for further tests. It was then discovered that the cancer was no longer spreading through her body but was confined to a small area. Radiation treatment was possible, though it had to wait because Muriel, with typical spirit, insisted that she and Bill first go on a holiday they had booked in Turkey.

"I feel that the treatment from Finbarr got me to the stage where I could have radiation," Muriel says, "and the doctor told me I had a fifty-fifty chance – whereas before I'd had none."

At the end of the radiation, tests revealed another problem and the possibility of an exploratory operation was discussed. This time, Muriel didn't hesitate. She immediately went back to Finbarr for a further set of treatments. She had more reaction after the second treatment, and felt ill for a time after this session. When she went for further check-ups it was found that there was no cause for alarm and the doctors decided not to operate. The doctors said that she need only

166

come for quarterly check-ups, and as time passed this in turn was phased down to half-yearly check-ups. She is now on annual check-ups, and the original ordeal is five years behind her.

When the doctor who had diagnosed the cancer came to the restaurant recently, Muriel and Bill presented him with a bottle of champagne. "You thought I was a crazy man, didn't you," Bill said to the doctor.

"You know, it's like a miracle," the doctor admitted. He never knew that Muriel had been to Finbarr.

Muriel and Bill feel very strongly that Finbarr was a vital part in the cure. The doctors could treat Muriel only at a point which was a consequence of his first treatment. An operation was being considered until after the second treatment. Finbarr himself thinks that this is one case where faith-healing could have had a part – the Bowens' own faith in themselves and in life. For their part, Muriel and Bill feel deep gratitude for the fact that Finbarr's gift could help.

"There's no way of proving that he cured me," Muriel said, "but I feel in myself that I'm here because of Finbarr."

LILY KELLY

Charnwood Estate, Bray, County Wicklow

Lily started having migraine headaches when she was fifteen years old. Soon she was having three or four a week, and they could each last up to six hours. The pain was so extreme that she would literally bang her head off the wall trying to make it go away. The condition is hereditary – her mother had it and her sister still has it.

She went to doctor after doctor. Each prescribed different medicines, but nothing relieved the condition. She was told to stop eating a range of foods, but again the problem persisted. The traditional routine of lying in a dark room when suffering from a migraine headache didn't help her either, and the problem was having a devastating effect on her life. Lily couldn't read when she had the headaches, she would feel nauseous, and she couldn't travel any distance because she might have an attack.

Lily found that two factors often triggered the headaches – certain smells such as perfumes, and any stressful situation.

During pregnancy, Lily wouldn't take any medicines and so her migraine became even more disruptive. When Lily was pregnant with her second child, however, the condition became even more extreme. After the birth of her third child, the headaches were making her life a misery.

She had read about Finbarr Nolan and, many years before, her mother had gone to a seventh son in Bray and had been cured of a skin condition. She then heard that Finbarr was

168

going to hold clinics at the Royal Hotel in Bray. Since conventional medicine had done nothing to help her, Lily decided to go to him.

Lily went with her aunt, who was suffering from arthritis. She also saw a woman she knew at the clinic who had brought along her young son who was suffering from a very severe skin rash.

When Finbarr treated Lily, she felt a burning sensation that she believed was healing her condition. "I felt as if it was being lifted out of my head," she says, "and that it was gone."

Lily believed in Finbarr's healing, and she was sure that she had been cured after the first visit. She hadn't had a headache when the time came for her second visit and she only went to that and the third visit to be sure of the cure. In the fifteen years since being treated by Finbarr, Lily hasn't suffered a single migraine headache. "The next time I went to my family doctor I told him Finbarr Nolan had cured my migraine headaches. He laughed, and said it was just a coincidence and that I'd simply grown out of them."

Lily's aunt also had a significant amount of relief from her arthritis after being treated by Finbarr, although the condition wasn't cured completely. Years later Lily met the woman who had been at the clinic with her son. She informed Lily that the boy's rash had healed completely after Finbarr's treatment. Lily's sister, unfortunately, hasn't tried a treatment by Finbarr and continues to suffer from migraine.

MARGARET HIGGINS

Cartonbrack, Kenagh, County Longford

In 1987 a woman and her teenage daughter arrived at a clinic in Carrick-on-Shannon to thank Finbarr for a cure that had taken place fifteen years before. When Margaret Higgins was two-and-a-half years old, her mother, Maire, had been convinced to bring her to Finbarr. At that time he was based in Arvagh and there were crowds flocking to him. Maire only brought her child for two visits, but that was enough to change everything.

Maire was six months' pregnant when she was rushed from Longford to Dublin. She gave birth to a daughter weighing only two pounds. Baby Margaret was kept in an incubator in the hospital for four months, and when Maire took her home she began to realise there was something different about her daughter.

"With the others, you'd put them in the cot or the pram and they'd be kicking the covers off," she said. "But with Margaret that never happened. She'd wave her hands, but she never moved her legs."

It wasn't that the legs were stiff or in some way disfigured. They were simply lifeless. They wouldn't hold the child's weight if she was held on someone's lap. They never moved at all.

When Maire went back to the hospital she had to deal with a specialist that she found far from helpful. She was distraught by the idea that her daughter mightn't be able to walk, and never fully grasped what was believed to be the problem. As the visits continued and the condition didn't change, tests were carried out on Margaret, and Maire was informed that the baby was of above average intelligence.

"I remember one time sitting crying and all the specialist had to say was that I should be thankful my baby was so intelligent," she recalls.

Finally, when Margaret was two-and-a-half years old, the specialist suggested putting callipers on the child's legs and Maire was to be informed when a cot would be free in the hospital to take Margaret in. Maire became ill around that time herself and she postponed the arrangement until she had recovered. In the meantime, however, Margaret's god-father had heard about Finbarr Nolan and was sure he could help. Maire couldn't see how Finbarr could make any differ-ence, but her friend insisted and so they went for two visits in the same week – Monday and Thursday.

There were huge crowds in Arvagh and Finbarr was very busy. "I don't think I've seen such crowds in all my life." Maire says, "The town itself was crowded and inside the hall was packed."

Finbarr treated Margaret very quickly, running his right hand along her hips and legs. Maire says she'll never forget what happened the following Sunday. "A nephew of my husband's was here and he lifted her out of the pram," she explains, "and Margaret started catching him by the shirt and pulling herself up. I said, 'She'll fall!' but as soon as he put her down she started climbing up again."

Maire watched in amazement as the nephew then propped Margaret at his feet and put a jar near her. She started reaching for it, and then she moved forward and crawled over to it. Maire burst into tears at the sight.

From then on, Margaret's improvement was rapid and Maire proudly showed to all who came to the house that her child was healthy and moving. The visits to Finbarr happened at the end of March, and in August Margaret was walking on her own.

Maire eventually went back to the specialist, fulfilling a previously arranged appointment, and told him that Finbarr Nolan had cured her daughter. The doctor made no comment. "As far as they were concerned they were finished with the matter – I was supposed to have kept with the doctors and not gone anywhere else."

In the years since, Maire has recommended many people to go to Finbarr. Margaret, now twenty-three years old, remains grateful to him for the fact that her life is normal. Finbarr himself is delighted at the fact that the family came back to him to let him know about this cure.

VERONICA CAMPBELL

The Burrow, Portrane, County Dublin

Veronica had psoriasis from the age of eleven. The skin ailment caused her a great deal of discomfort and embarrassment. "My knees were the worst with the problem," she explained, "and had a layer almost half an inch thick. My hair was very bad too. I couldn't comb it and I was ashamed to go to a hairdresser. The disease was all over my body – my ears were always cut, and it was even down my forehead and through my eyebrows."

She couldn't wear the clothes she wanted to – dressing instead to hide the problem all the time. She was treated in Hume Street Hospital for many years, and had tried many different creams and treatments. These would sometimes ease the psoriasis a little, but never cured it. People would advise her to get plenty of sun, but in her case this only made the rash redder. She was told that the problem would ease, at least during pregnancy, but even this wasn't the case.

Veronica was in her early twenties when she went to Finbarr Nolan in 1974. It was Finbarr's first clinic on the north side of Dublin. There were hundreds of people there including, she recalls, two young women who had very extreme psoriasis. That helped Veronica not to feel too self-conscious. She was impressed by Finbarr. He was so young and he was quiet and pleasant. "He was just like a doctor," she said. "He looked at the problem, treated me, and there was no attempt by him

173

to get me into any particular frame of mind. I found him very nice and very relaxed."

Veronica's mother also believed in Finbarr, and had been treated by him for a minor ailment. Veronica was in many ways determined that the treatment would work. "I knew nothing else was going to cure it – I had tried everything – and I went to Finbarr believing he was going to cure me. As he was touching me he seemed to be praying, and I was praying along with him hoping I'd be cured."

Finbarr has talked in his own recollections of the fact that his hands feel different to certain people. Certainly, with Veronica, there was a very definite effect which she felt. "The first night I went, he touched me from my feet up and I felt nothing. The second time I went back, it was unbelievable. He was only touching me lightly, but somehow it felt as if he was squeezing me together. I felt as if something was being driven out through the top of my head by some power. I had gone with a nephew of mine, and I asked him if he'd felt anything – he said he hadn't. But the feeling I had was unbelievable. I think he cured me at that stage. I went back a third time, but felt nothing unusual. I felt so affected by the second visit that I forgot even to look at the psoriasis. Where I had the problem only slightly, it faded fairly soon. By about two or three months later, my psoriasis had completely vanished. I've never had the problem since."

It was a liberation for her, and she could dress as she wished and feel good about herself again. "I could start wearing mini-skirts at last," she joked.

Veronica's daughter, Paula, also developed psoriasis – though less extreme than her mother – around the age of twelve. She, too, had tried all the usual treatments. When she was nineteen, she went to Finbarr three times. "I told her to believe in him and he'd cure her," Veronica said.

But Paula wasn't convinced. "I didn't have much faith in him, and I certainly didn't have the kind of attitude towards him that my mother had," she explained. "The third time, when I came out my legs were shaking and I felt strange. But there was no cure. It was early summer and I was about to go away on holiday and I got a sunbed treatment just before leaving. The psoriasis improved during the holiday and went away for a few weeks, but then it came back."

As we were coming to the close of the interview, I mentioned to Veronica the case Finbarr had described where a woman with psoriasis had come to him but allowed him only to touch certain parts of her body. She came back months later because the areas he had touched were cured but the others weren't. It transpired that the very same thing happened to Veronica. "There's one part he didn't touch and the psoriasis is still there," she laughed heartily. Her conclusion about Finbarr was unequivocal: "He definitely has healing powers," she said, "and thank God it worked on me and cured me."

RODNEY SIMPSON

Armagh, Northern Ireland

Recently Rodney sprained his ankle while playing football one lunchtime with his workmates. He went to the casualty department of the local hospital, gave his name, and sat down to join the queue. Medical staff rushed out to the waiting-room and hurried Rodney in on full alert until he explained to them that it was just his ankle that was bothering him. In previous years, his name had become synonymous with life and death emergencies.

Finbarr's treatments have given relief and have even saved lives. The cure of Rodney was a liberation for the young man himself and for the entire family.

When Rodney Simpson was three years old he started developing a chest complaint. His parents brought him to the doctor, and it transpired that he had asthma. He started getting treatment for the condition, and was prescribed ventolin. Over the following years, the condition continued. It meant that he couldn't join in games with other children and that he didn't do very well in his studies, and it required his parents to be on the alert day and night. "Even in those early days it was something that bothered me every single day," he says.

When Rodney was seventeen, however, something happened that made his asthma life-threatening. The asthma was making him feel ill one day in school, and he informed a teacher who said he should go to the sick-room where he would be tended to if he didn't feel better after ten minutes. Incredibly, the staff forgot about him and he was left alone there for two hours. He became so weak that he barely managed to drag himself out of the room. He was spotted then by a teacher who realised that the emergency was so great there was no time to wait for the ambulance which was on its way. She drove Rodney to the hospital.

"By the time he got to the hospital he was almost dead," Rodney's father told me.

He was rushed into intensive care and his heart stopped before he could respond to treatment. He was then kept unconscious on a ventilator and after a week it was found that he still wasn't breathing properly for himself. He was kept unconscious this way for seventeen days in all, and a special mask to get more oxygen into Rodney's body had to be devised before he finally started recovering.

From then onwards, his asthma attacks became extreme. They would either come so quickly he could hardly respond to save himself, or else warning signs would haunt him for days without a full-scale attack. The attacks could happen at any time, and they always required hospital attention.

"I was in and out of hospital on average four times a year after that incident in 1986," Rodney explains. He never lasted in jobs because of his sick record, and he was often moody and depressed because he felt so weak. His parents had to be constantly watchful of him, and his mother remembers many sleepless nights listening for him to call out if he seemed unwell when going to bed.

Rodney's mother saw an advertisement about Finbarr coming to the area and she suggested going, although she left the final decision to Rodney. He said he wanted to go.

"It seemed like a lost cause, because the best medication in the world didn't help me," he says. Nevertheless he went. "I felt that Finbarr could be the means by which God would answer my prayers and cure me if I truly believed and I truly wanted to be healed."

He experienced a great sense of power surging into him at each treatment, and he felt as if Finbarr was dragging the illness out. The sensation was stronger with each treatment. At the end of the three visits, Finbarr warned Rodney that he might get worse before getting better. A month after his treatments Rodney had an attack which was so severe he suffered respiratory arrest and was on a life-support machine.

That was in March 1990. Rodney hasn't had an asthma attack since. He got a new job in the April of that year and has kept it ever since because his attendance hasn't been disrupted. The whole atmosphere in the home changed, because Rodney was more cheerful and energetic and his parents could stop worrying about his well-being. As he became obviously stronger and more independent, he started reaching out for the natural experiences that had been denied him – going away on holidays, getting involved in physical exercise, devoting spare time to charity work, and finally moving into a home of his own.

"In many ways I had an over-protected youth," Rodney tells me, "but since the changes in my life after I saw Finbarr I've built up my own confidence and my parents don't have to worry about me either. It's a great peace of mind. For me, it's a changed life."

"It's like Finbarr helped the whole family," Rodney's mother says.

"There was a time when we feared if Rodney was going to come falling in the door or if we were going to get a phone call saying he'd had an attack," his father adds. "Now he comes in the door whistling."

There was a side-effect of the last asthma attack, however, which a further set of treatments from Finbarr hasn't cured:

Rodney has alopecia. He again felt a very strong power coming from Finbarr, and the treatment gave signs of hair growth. But Rodney then went back to using the medicine he had been prescribed to treat the hair-loss and the new hair fell out. He remains hopeful of a cure through a further set of treatments from Finbarr, but the alopecia means nothing to him compared to the suffering he endured from asthma.

"Asthma made me different from the crowd because I couldn't do the things other people could do," Rodney smiles. "Now I'm able to go out and do the things everyone can do and having alopecia means that I'm the first person noticed in the crowd."

TWO STUDIES

Finbarr has always been open to any test examining his healing. To date, however, only two tests have been conducted, and of these only one was fully completed and documented.

The brief account by Dr Jack Kapchen of the Department of Psychology at the University of Miami at least demonstrates the respect Finbarr gained through their work together.

The more comprehensive work carried out by Dr Robert Willner, however, presents plain facts which fit very well with Finbarr's own claims in terms of success-rate and his cures having nothing to do with faith-healing.

JACK A. KAPCHEN Ph.D.

University of Miami
Department of Psychology

I first met Finbarr Nolan about ten years ago. I had heard him as a guest on *The Larry King Show* and was very impressed with his humility and low-key approach. He made no exaggerated claims about his "powers" but rather dispassionately related his experiences and background. He pointed out that in certain cultures being the seventh son of a seventh son almost automatically bestowed psychic powers on that individual. From childhood on, people were bringing sick relatives, friends and even animals to be healed. He stated that he did what he could to help and soon found that "laying on of hands" seemed to increase positive outcomes. What was particularly impressive was that Finbarr made no attempt to theorise, hypothesise, or explain the phenomena. He accepted the fact that there might be psychological factors involved, but did not attempt to rationalise his work in terms of spiritual, religious or metaphysical "gifts". He stated that if what he did helped some people, that was enough and he would leave it to the "experts" to explain it.

When Finbarr came to Miami and Fort Lauderdale, I got in touch with him and asked him if he would participate in some studies and experiments. He was most cordial and co-operative, and we performed some preliminary studies. We also did some psychological evaluations, which, although fragmentary, gave no indication of any psychopathology.

Unfortunately, we never completed the studies because Finbarr had other commitments that took him out of Florida.

About a year later, I was asked to be the consultant for a workshop on "Psychic Powers and Neurolinguistic Programming". I had recommended Finbarr and Uri Geller as the "models". Unfortunately, Geller had other commitments and was unable to participate. The organisers of the week-long workshop had also contacted other "psychics" who had achieved some "New Age" notoriety. As the workshop proceeded it became evident that Finbarr was the only subject who merited credibility. The others were treated with scepticism and rejection. What also impressed me was that, during our free time, Finbarr attempted healing anyone and everyone that was presented to him.

At this point, parapsychology is a most controversial subject. Unorthodox healing is perhaps the most controversial area within this field. The recent scandals have made "faith-healing" even less credible. Yet, within medical and psychological research, the whole area of mind-body healing, psychoneuroimmunology, has become a major interest. It may well be that individuals like Finbarr Nolan need to be studied more intensively, perhaps with funded research, by orthodox science that can provide the insights that are so crucial to an understanding of these phenomena. In Finbarr Nolan we have someone who also has achieved some success in his endeavours, yet continues to say, "Here I am. If I can help you understand the dynamics of mind-body interaction through what I do, that would be my greatest reward."

January 1992

26 AUGUST, 1981

To whom it may concern:

I am presenting to you a clinical summary of an experiment that I performed in my office in the late 1980s.

Ten patients were followed in this office twice a week for two weeks for the purpose of observation only. The patients were informed clearly that no treatment was involved and that they were simply being evaluated for participation in an experiment which involved a new medication for their condition. All of these patients had not responded to many attempts of therapy for their condition. Finbarr Nolan, a "touch-healer", masqueraded in the office as a medical intern and simply examined the patients on the four occasions under my direction. None of the patients were aware of the true identity of Finbarr Nolan. At the fourth visit, nine of the patients (one dropped out of the experiment) were questioned as to the current state of health and the status of their medical problems. The results were as follows:

> two patients completely free of all symptomology.
> three patients 50 per cent improved or better.
> four patients no change.

I do not attempt to claim the outcome as a relationship of cause and effect. I simply present the results of a rather fascinating experiment. This in no way should be interpreted as an endorsement of Finbarr Nolan. I do think that this presentation certainly suggests that further investigation could have merit.

Respectfully submitted,

Robert E. Willner, MD

MEDICAL ARTICLE

Laying on of hands

As a medical student I was taught that the laying on of hands is an important means of communication. This gesture is designed to establish contact with the patient on both a psychological and physical basis. I have been aware for twenty-five years that touching my patients is essential if I am going to instil in them the feeling of confidence, trust and security in our relationship. I was reminded of this one day in August 1980 while dining at a friend's restaurant. I was introduced to Mr Finbarr Nolan who is well known in Europe as a "touch-healer". My friends and I spent a fascinating evening discussing Mr Nolan's background and his accomplishments. This remarkable young man has been "touch-healing" since he was a young child. What captured my attention most was that there was no religious connotation to his technique. My curiosity was aroused. I suggested that we set up an experiment in my office to test the abilities of this young man. We established the protocol that night: Mr Nolan was to be introduced to my patients as Dr Finn, a student from the medical school in Dublin, Ireland. I have taught many medical students over the years and it is not an uncommon sight to have a student assisting me in my examinations in the office. The patients were told that Dr Finn was assisting me in an experiment. The first part of this experiment involved the observation of a patient for three visits a week over a period of two weeks, so as to establish the normal course of their disease and to determine if any unusual patterns existed. Ten patients were selected on the basis of the severity of their disease and their failure to respond to multiple attempts at medical therapy. The patients were told that we did not know what the second portion of the experiment would be until the first portion was completed. It was explained that the rôle of the medical student was to confirm my observation and to make observations of his own, thus providing two separate evaluations of the patient's disease process.

Observation and examination of the patients was begun on 9 September 1980. Mr Nolan explained to me that he required at least three touchings and that it involved placing his hands on the areas where the disease or the pain existed. A brief summary of each case and their progress follows:

Case No. 1: Female, 30 years of age; Chart #1393.
CHIEF COMPLAINT: Constant alternating constipation and diarrhoea with frequent blood in the stool.
DIAGNOSIS: Chronic Ulcerative Colitis (confirmed both by sigmoidoscopy and X-ray). The patient has been under the care of gastroenterologists for many years with occasional remissions. She also had a confirmed diagnosis of chronic interstitial cystitis.
PROGRESS: After the first visit the patient's colitis came under control. There was no diarrhoea, constipation or bleeding. The cystitis did not improve. The patient remained symptom-free for several weeks following her last "touching" on 30 September 1980.

Case No. 2: Female, 60 years of age; Chart #1445
CHIEF COMPLAINT: Shortness of breath and wheezing due to asthmatic bronchitis for 23 years. She has had post-traumatic arthritic pains in the right ankle, left leg and thigh and knees since 1971.

COMMENTS: The patient had been using Mistometer, a medicated inhaler, Theodur and Tedral when she first came to the office. She stated that her pain complaints were usually most severe while working.

PROGRESS: 11 September: Pains 50 per cent better, asthma improved 50 per cent, but was worse on occasion.

16 September: Patient is using the Mistometer less, having milder attacks, feels that she is 50 per cent better. Pain in the left knee and thigh worse. Pain in the feet and ankle worse.

18 September: Pain behind the knee and calf the same. The feet and the knees 90 per cent better. The patient is not using any medication at all for the asthma and feels much better. At this visit, the patient was told about Finbarr Nolan and who he was.

23 September: Markedly improved. No wheezing.

7 October: No wheeze since 30 September. No pains.

Case No. 3: Male, 56 years of age; Chart #1701

CHIEF COMPLAINTS: Anxiety and depression for twenty-one years. Coldness of the body for 1 to 2 years, fear on awakening, complains that he cannot take criticism, has generalised body aches, loses his temper easily and has pains in his ears. The patient is currently on Librium 25 mg one to four times a day along with Pertofrane. He has been under the care of a psychiatrist for many years, though he has not visited psychiatrist for over a month.

PROGRESS: 11 September: Depression in the morning, conflicting feelings about work, no change in condition, increased fear in ability to teach, is losing his temper less, increased feelings of helplessness. Aches and pains are gone, less tendency to cry.

16 September: Patient under stress because fear of loss of job; everything seems worse. However, his temper was better.

18 September: The patient felt a little better this morning, still has problems, was told about Finbarr Nolan.

186

7 October: Patient feels that he has been helped a little overall. States that he felt "energy" when he was touched by Finbarr Nolan.

Case No. 4: Details unknown.
CHIEF COMPLAINTS: Right arm and neck pain for one year. Bad taste in the mouth, has frequent nervous blinking of the eyes.

DIAGNOSIS: Post-traumatic cervical arthritis. The patient seen by neurologist and no help affects from therapy.

PROGRESS: 16 September: Improved except for blinking of the eyes. Subjectively the patient did not feel this, however, objectively it was noted that there was less blinking.

23 September: Eyes unchanged.

2 October: Eyes improved. At this time the patient was informed as to who Finbarr Nolan was. It should be noted that the patient was at the same time under treatment with acupuncture for the other conditions which did relieve the bad taste in the mouth and the arm and neck pain. However, no treatment was given for the eyes other than the "touching" of Finbarr Nolan.

Case No. 5: Details unknown.
CHIEF COMPLAINTS: Pain and spasm in the left hand.

DIAGNOSIS: Post-surgical spinal trauma. The patient has been under the care of a phychiatrist (specialist in physical medicine and rehabilitation) for one year.

PROGRESS: 11 September: No change in the pain and spasm at the base of the neck, the left hand, anterior thigh and the side of the right thigh and the posterior aspect of the right leg.

16 September: Patient was worse for one night then no change. Pain persists in both hands, buttocks and hips.

18 September: No change. Patient informed of Finbarr Nolan.

22 September: No change.

30 September: Better this morning.

7 October: No change at all.

Case No. 6: Female, 59 years of age; Chart #unknown.

CHIEF COMPLAINTS: Severe depression over past five to six years. Tremors, history of seizures. Patient had seizure on the morning of the first visit prior to arriving at the office. Had another seizure one week before.

DIAGNOSIS: Chronic depression and ventricular cyst (brain cyst). Current medication: Patient was on Corgard 40 mg daily.

PROGRESS: 11 September: The patient related that the day after the treatment she was worse but was now better and stated that she would like to be with her family.

16 September: 80 per cent better than she was the first day. 40 per cent better compared to 8 years ago. Improvement in appetite and depression.

18 September: No further change. Told about Finbarr Nolan.

7 October: Patient no better, however the acute episode had subsided.

Case No. 7: Female, 81 years of age; Chart #6.

CHIEF COMPLAINT: Shortness of breath since having had the flu in 1918, weakness.

DIAGNOSIS: Chronic obstructive pulmonary disease, pulmonary fibrosis, asthmatic bronchitis and hypertensive cardiovascular disease. The patient has been under the care of a respiratory specialist, takes oxygen at home and is on Theophyllin and Lasix.

PROGRESS: 11 September: Legs very weak, muscles ache, breathing the same. Had been without oxygen. However this is unusual.

16 September: Fell on 11 September because legs were weak. Depressed, shortness of breath and wheezing. Appetite less, pulse 96, not active because of wheezing.

23 September: Worse than ever, shortness of breath; wheezing less, however.

8 October: No change.

Case No. 8: Male, 63 years of age; Chart #1433

CHIEF COMPLAINT: Tinnitus (ringing in the ears).

DIAGNOSIS: Cerebral vascular accident (stroke), pituitary tumour and tinnitus. The patient has been under the care of a neurologist. The patient had been receiving acupuncture in my office which improved most of the patient's complaints except for the ringing in the ears. The patient seen on two subsequent occasions – 22 September and 16 October. The tinnitus persisted; however, the patient spontaneously commented that "that young man had a very strange touch and made me very relaxed".

Case No. 9: Female, 52 years of age; Chart #2679

CHIEF COMPLAINTS: Fatigue, shortness of breath and depression. Cannot stop eating, needs something in the mouth all the time, needs to chew solids.

DIAGNOSIS: Morbid obesity, hypertension, arteriosclerotic heart disease. Medication: Digoxin, Quinaglute, anti-depressants. Patient did not respond in any way to the touching of Finbarr Nolan.

Case No. 10: Male, 68 years of age; Chart #8009

CHIEF COMPLAINT: Pain on the left side of the face, left ear painful. Condition began with a rash on 18 August 1980 and has persisted.

DIAGNOSIS: Herpes Zoster. The patient has been seen in consultation by a dermatologist and has not responded to the medications or therapies administered.

PROGRESS: 9 September: When first seen the patient had painful scabbing around the left ear, cheek, scalp and neck.

11 September: No pain yesterday. The patient slept well, having a little pain today in the left cheek and along the side of the head.

16 September: Patient having left-temporal headaches, pain in the left side of the neck, more during the night and less during the day. The face feels much better.

18 September: Headaches are gone, the face is healing better. There is no pain.

22 September: Headaches less, patient sleeps better. The patient commented that his hands, which were stiff when he first came into the office, are 90 per cent better. He has no pain in the face or ear at all.

GENERAL COMMENTS: It is important to note that during the time in which these patients were seen, no therapy of any kind was administered. Only brief questioning and simple examination of the patient was performed. Four of the ten patients were completely unaffected by the examinations; five patients showed definite response of a positive nature and the improvement was thought to be of a significant nature, in some cases 60 per cent to 100 per cent improvement. Two of these cases were extremely difficult and showed dramatic results. One case improved with reference to the acute symptomatology, but maintained the chronic depressed attitude that had existed for approximately five years. It is also important to note that all of these patients have been under the care of extremely fine specialists in the fields to which their diseases were related. Except for the increased attention that the patients were getting, I am not aware of any other positive influencing factor on the progress of the disease in any of them. One would expect that a patient in this setting would continue with their symptomatology in the hope that they would be chosen for the continuation of the experiment because their symptoms persisted. The usual reason for being included in an experiment is that your disease has been unsuccessfully treated up to this point and, therefore, a good choice for something new. The patients were not charged for their visits. Therefore, monetary incentive was absent. Placebo effect cannot be included here because no therapy was offered. It would certainly be expected that the absence of such an offering of help or treatment would have a negative effect, if any, on the overall outcome of the experiment.

I do not believe in magic, but I do believe that there is a rational explanation for all phenomenon. It would be easy to speculate that the phenomenon observed here was coincidental, perhaps due to magnetic fields, biochemical factors, and so on. Speculation, however, serves no purpose except to point the way to possible avenues of investigation.

I do not wish to speculate. I wish only to point out that a very definite phenomenon appears to have occurred when Finbarr Nolan performed his "touch healing". I am convinced from my limited experience with this young man that some process did occur and that this process demands investigation. Medicine can only profit from understanding this phenomenon and utilising it for the benefit of patients. I have been reminded that the laying on of hands may be far more beneficial than I ever before had suspected.